prison
break

Mending Review

☐ Adult   ☐ YA   ☐ Children's

Please check problem and describe if applicable:

☑ Needs new label

☐ Torn/loose pages #

☐ Split binding (needs glue/reinforcement)

☐ Needs new jacket (books) or case (A/V)

☐ Problem with disc/track #_____

☐ Other _____

Consider replacing. The following cannot be repaired:

☐ Poor condition—worn, yellow, brittle, stained

☐ Missing page or part of page #

☐ Sewn or spiral binding split/loose

Initials/Date: K (/10-23-23

prison break

True Stories of the World's Greatest Escapes

PAUL BUCK

JB

JOHN BLAKE

Published by John Blake Publishing Ltd,
3 Bramber Court, 2 Bramber Road,
London W14 9PB, England

www.johnblakepublishing.co.uk

www.facebook.com/Johnblakepub

twitter.com/johnblakepub

First published as *the E-list* for Pennant Books in 2008.
This edition published in paperback in 2012

ISBN: 978-1-84358-960-0

British Library Cataloguing-in-Publication Data:

A catalogue record for this book is available from the British Library.

Design by www.envydesign.co.uk

Printed and bound by CPI Group (UK) Ltd, Croydon, CR0 4YY

1 3 5 7 9 10 8 6 4 2

© Text copyright Paul Buck 2012

Papers used by John Blake Publishing are natural, recyclable products made from
wood grown in sustainable forests. The manufacturing processes conform to the
environmental regulations of the country of origin.

Every attempt has been made to contact the relevant copyright-holders,
but some were unobtainable. We would be grateful if the appropriate
people could contact us.

Contents

ACKNOWLEDGEMENTS

On a broad level, my thanks extend to all those books, newspapers, magazines and website resources that I have used for research, not only in recent times but over the years. Many are found in my own library, but I have also turned to the London Borough of Bexley's libraries, and thank all those employed there – particularly in Sidcup and Central Library – for their efforts, including their search for books which were catalogued but seemed to have gone walkabout or escaped.

I would also like to acknowledge here three different friendships dating back to the 1970s: Paul Walton, the sociologist, who in those heady days turned me onto media studies, the issue of deviancy, and *Psychological Survival*, the research work from Durham Prison that was plainly helpful to Walter Probyn, John McVicar and others; Roger Jean Ségalat, in Lausanne, who involved me in factual crime writing; and, in Paris, Jean-Patrick Manchette, with whom I shared hours of dialogue and correspondence on crime and crime writing.

Back further, perhaps I should note my class year at a Catholic grammar school in the late fifties and early sixties for opening my eyes to criminal matters and helping to create my own inclinations, way before I discovered ideas through Colin Wilson, Albert Camus and Georges Bataille, to name but a few barbed wires.

To return to this particular book: my thanks to Cass Pennant, the publisher, who responded directly to my proposition; to Paul Woods, who instigated my involvement, helped pursue contacts, and indeed provided an interview that gives fresh information, as well as making editorial contributions; to others, some of whom are named in the text but who may not want to be named here – though I think Patsy Fleming, Dennis Woods, Terry Dunford, Beryl Smith and Terry Smith will not mind being credited for their help. And thanks also to Colin Lane for coming to the rescue over a problematic tape.

And finally to my wife, Catherine, who, as always, helped with my research and also diligently read and contributed to all aspects of what I've written. To her, my deep gratitude and love. This book is dedicated to her.

OVER THE WALLS
AND FAR AWAY

As the prisons of Britain grow desperately overcrowded, now is the time to consider escape. In fact, it would be morally irresponsible *not* to consider it, for when the authorities state that they must break the rules, the safety limits, to house all their miscreants, it becomes necessary to talk about escape as a way to safeguard the mental and physical wellbeing of those incarcerated in our prisons.

Unless, that is, you wish merely to damn them and leave them to their lot. If so, this is not the book for you.

Perhaps, too, we should reconsider the point of additional sentences for those recaptured after their escapes, unless they have committed other offences in the process. In some countries, it is legally acceptable to seek to escape because it is regarded as only human to do so.

The focus of this book is notorious escapes, or 'great escapes', but only those of civilian prisoners. The idea is not to document escapes from the PoW camps of World War Two, for example, no matter how spectacular and heart-stopping many of them happen to be. Undoubtedly, we think of the Great Escape itself, Colditz and the Wooden Horse as part of our history, so much so that the accounts of civilian escapees since 1946 regularly refer to those historic wartime episodes, either because they were inspired to take on board particular details for their own escapes, or because the spirit and courage of the wartime escapees have fired successive prisoners with a sense of their own personal challenge. Steve McQueen in *The Great Escape* echoes through so many of their stories that his image, leaping the first fence on a motorbike, would not have been out of place on this book's cover – even if no one here has taken that course of action as a mode of escape.

That said, I have included the IRA (Irish Republican Army) because, though a paramilitary organisation, their crimes were resolutely regarded as criminal rather than political, and thus, on the British government's own terms, they have every right to be included here. (Another approach might have included those who escaped over the Berlin Wall during the Cold War, as one could view the Eastern Bloc on the whole as a prison.)

Our focus on civilian prisoners indicates that the escapees are those incarcerated for crimes, mainly robbery or murder. However, in general, I have rarely dwelt on the details of how those included found themselves in custody, unless it becomes necessary to the narrative. Likewise, the structure of London gangland, for example, is barely taken into account, as these matters are not particularly relevant to this work.

My intention has been to explore *how* the prisoner escaped, not to pursue the reason why. That would be another book in itself, and would include such reasons as: refusal of permission to attend a family funeral; to spend a few days with the family, wife or girlfriend, particularly if there was turbulence in the relationship; to prove one's innocence; or to carry out a job that's been lined up which will set the prisoner up for life (or so he hopes) – as well as the fundamental reason that *people do not want to be imprisoned*. Such a book would also have to explore strategies and stratagems to prevent escape.

This is a book about the escapee who thinks of little other than escape from the moment he is confined, as well as those who take the opportunity when it arises … be it a rope dangling over the prison wall or a door left unlocked, or open.

Why some people should escape while others do not is far from discernible. Some prisoners have observed that if someone is imprisoned for short spells they tend not to try to escape, whereas those same people may react more dramatically against a long sentence. Perhaps there is no real answer, but we can glean an insight or two as we examine individual cases.

Alfred Hinds, a master of escaping, summed up his observations thus: "The vast majority of prisoners are resigned if not content to do their bird. Some will escape if the chance is handed to them on a plate. But all they want is a brief taste of freedom; for instance, the chance to spend a few days with their wife or girl-friend. It usually is a brief taste, because they have no organisation and it's almost a relief to them when they're recaptured. Then there's a small hard core of determined men who will plan an escape and go through with it. These are usually prisoners with long sentences of P.D. [preventive detention] but nothing to come out to. If a professional criminal has managed to salt away some loot, he'll accept a sentence of five years or even more. If he hasn't, he'll want to get out and pull off a big job, after which he won't mind too much being re-arrested. In his curious logic, he accepts his sentence as a just reward. The snag is that, if caught, he gets another and longer term of imprisonment."

This book has primarily been an adventure in unravelling the different approaches to escape. I am not sure that, like many an escapee, I knew where it would lead, if I would draw any conclusions, or if I would end up back at the beginning. But I suspected that, in the process, I would discover something about my attitude to the issues raised. Perhaps one cannot ask for more. Perhaps this is what I want for the reader.

Here you will find escapes that begin in the cell, the showers, the laundry, the mailroom, the yard. Here you will discover those who go over the wall, under the wall, through the gate. Here you will see helicopters at work, or transit vehicles brought to a halt. Here you will find the planned escape, as well as the opportune escape. And you will witness the escape of the loner who does not require the involvement of others – or that of the escapee who requires help from fellow inmates, or from an insider, like a corrupt officer providing tools or weapons. Or from the friends and relatives who smuggle in requested items, or provide getaway cars.

Any notion of strict categorisation does not work, for the encyclopaedic method hinders readability. One slight regret is that I had to cut back for the sake of length, to take away some of the details of the planning, the frustration, the perseverance noted by the escapees themselves, even if the sheer number of cases does convey a further dimension. It has not been my job to plot every move until recapture … or, indeed, the lives afterwards of those who are not recaptured.

One of the remarkable factors to emerge time and time again is the amount of care, attention and energy given to an escape, only to see it fizzle into a sketchy series of possibilities once the escapee gets his leg over the wall. Not everyone has plans, beyond the plan to get away. They may not know where they will hide, where they will run to, or how they will continue to stay out. Some, as noted, are really only going out for a short break, perhaps only intending to see their families, knowing they will be quickly recaptured. Some have money available from their crimes to flee abroad, for there are still countries where no extradition treaties are fully operational. For many years it was the Spanish coastline, the 'Costa del Crime', although that is not officially the case today. But extradition has not been retrospectively applied, and it is still a popular residence for escapees – probably because they can blend in more easily amongst the world of former criminals, as well as the general British contingent of ex-pats.

The use of the masculine 'he' is quite noticeable too, for all but a few escapes are by men. This is no gender bias on my part. I have included the few women I unearthed, though I could probably have found others. However, the intent was not to excavate for the sake of it, but rather to demonstrate the breadth and the resourcefulness of the escapees. Whilst I focus on some because of their distinctive aspects, I offer others to provide context. Likewise, whilst this study draws from a wealth of British cases, I give some perspective on other escapes from all around Europe and the rest of the world.

And whilst I didn't want to delve through history in any great depth, I felt that a handful of comparisons from the past would add another dimension. To escape today, in a practical sense, is very different from escaping thirty years ago – let alone three hundred years ago, even if, on another level, it is still the spirit of Man that is making that bid for freedom.

This is not an endless list of escapes all subjected to the same degree of analysis. What I wanted was to show the sheer bravado, the courage, the daring, that comprises the strength of the human spirit, which is to be cherished. And yes, I am aware that there are escapes that have led to further murders – indeed, I was horrified by some of the events as I read through them. But it is the spirit of Man that I am celebrating, through all his triumphs and adversities, without which mankind may well not survive.

I have refrained from getting too technical by categorising prisoners as A, B, C ... or the varying levels of risk classification, as 'standard escape risk', 'high escape risk' or 'exceptional escape risk', as these have changed over the years and across the different countries. In general, those who feature are prisoners who have escaped before and have the 'escape risk' label attached to their name, if not to their prison apparel. The term 'E-list' – 'escape-list' in UK Home Office terminology – is not intended as a restricting or defining term, as the ground covered goes way back before such official terminology was employed. However, these are all people who would have been on an 'E-list', people who made it their aim, or in some cases claimed it was their duty, to escape.

Though I am drawing on many angles for my information, the viewpoint that interests me the most has to come from those who have experienced escaping from prison. Whether their crimes are seen as horrendous, or more mainstream (albeit perhaps major); whether we have admired them for it, or been aghast at their further offences. But, at the end of the day, we, as readers, were not there, did not experience the fear and violence that stemmed from some of these men's actions. As Tommy Wisbey's daughter, Marilyn, notes in her autobiography, it's very romantic to read about them, but if you are in the midst of a robbery, whether being committed with guns or coshes, you never know if those weapons are going to be used.

This may come across as an intense book, because I've tried to trim away some of the frills; yet, at the same time, I wanted to preserve some of the character of those involved. There are no rules as to what I left in and what I took out. My desire was to keep you reading, to view the tragedies along with the humorous aspects, to add probable annoyance as well as offering possible justification.

But I did want to lean toward the side of the escapee, though not for any moralising purpose. Most criminals are not proud of being criminals. Some had a raw deal. Most knew what they were doing. That is not my concern. I wanted to give their stories because *they* were the ones locked in a cell for years on end. Many gave every waking hour, unless distracted, to focusing on escape.

We may pass comment on the neighbour who locks their dog in a kitchen whilst they go to work. We might empathise with the poor beast whining away. And yet we don't want to give much thought to the human being who is locked away, and who does not make much noise … or, if he does, we find ourselves unsympathetic. But if you condemn this man, then you condemn part of your own spirit.

The idea of escaping, or absconding, from prison – or indeed any form of custody, like transport vans, police stations, law courts – has been etched into our psyche in modern times by television and cinema, often making the event more spectacular, more thrilling, perhaps somewhat romantic. All the heroes are rugged and handsome, and it is probably no good for the real men in our prisons, who we cannot see – the gangsters, criminals, 'villains', hardmen – to be confused with film fantasies. For once they are out of prison, whether by escape or official release, they face the agonising temptation to continue as a recidivist rather than seek legitimate employment.

Walter Probyn turned away from the limelight. He may well recognise that he has become a famed escapee, but he says he was not a competent criminal and shouldn't be emulated. Unlike many others, Probyn wished his talents could have been developed and put to better use.

Bruce Reynolds (not an escapee himself, unlike some of his fellow Great Train Robbers) has a different perspective: "Perhaps it was like what happens when a footballer or mountaineer comes to the end of their career. They live their entire life on the edge, but what happens when it's all over, when you have to stop? It was very hard for … us when we quit. When we came out of jail we were old men, and too well known. We knew we had to stop for our families' sake. *But you never stop missing the buzz*." (My emphasis.)

Today's prisoners are faced with more sophisticated technology to prevent their escape. Everyone knows it will be more difficult. But then, at least one of the escapes in this book occurred less than six months ago as I write. If there is a weakness in the system, then the prisoner who is fixed on escaping, who is watching and scheming, will take advantage of it.

And the greatest weakness will always be the human element, the guards and officials who go about their job in a routine way and who slacken at their peril. Equipment might become faulty, a camera may go on the blink, but it is invariably the guard who just pops off to the toilet, who falls asleep, who engages in convivial conversation and is lulled into a false sense of security, who recurs repeatedly throughout these cases. The people who are employed as guards are hardly likely to be among the brightest, and the probability is that some of the prisoners are of substantially higher intelligence. Television programmes feed us a diet of crime fiction where video cameras are properly maintained and operated, which does not equate with reality. Talk to people who live near a prison and they will tell you that there are periods when escapes over the wall can become quite prolific. Those at fault fight hard to cover up their inadequacies in not having prevented them.

It's not that many years ago since the Chief Constable of Durham was offering scare headlines in relation to the Great Train Robbers housed in Durham Prison, suggesting these men and their associates would stop at nothing, "even to the extent of using tanks, bombs and what the Army describes as limited atomic weapons. Once armoured vehicles had breached the main gates there would be nothing to stop them. A couple of tanks could easily have come through the streets of Durham unchallenged." How flattering to the convicted men. One has the impression that the police chief was starring in his own movie: "If that happened there would be a pitched battle and a lot of people would be killed." He could have appeared alongside Robert Duvall on the beach in *Apocalypse Now*. Soldiers were posted with fixed bayonets. Extra police patrolled with dogs. But nothing materialised. No helicopters came swooping in. And he said he was trying to strip the criminals of their glamour!

In the first chapter, with Charlie Wilson, I've given greater detail to create some sense of the atmosphere and the conditions. But it has not been my intention to give all the details all the time. I have created rules, and I have transgressed those rules at every turn. I make no apologies. Books have been written by escapees like Hinds and Probyn not only to relate their habitual escapes, but also to explore the reasons behind them. This book has to make their cases brief in order to encompass many others. Some names have become famous by virtue of one escape, whilst others, like Patsy Fleming and Georgie Madson, are regularly mentioned but rarely given coverage. (Perhaps they were pleased to be out of the public eye, as it could have been an obvious hindrance at the time.)

Sometimes one has to suspend belief at some of the details, for fact has often been more extraordinary than fiction. Reading about some of those who appear within, notwithstanding some of their crimes, the spirit of these people in escaping from incarceration has been far more inspirational than any of the splurge of biographies that our celebrity culture pours out daily.

But our age of celebrity affects villains as much as anyone else. They are no different. The criminal is as much a part of society as a film star, a politician or a lawyer. (Or even a debt collector.)

Paul Buck

The master escapologist Harry Houdini is the perennial reference point for everybody who escapes more than a couple of times from prison, and who, like Houdini, is working at the limits and does what seems to be the impossible. But, just as most of us couldn't imagine ourselves as a Houdini, we also cannot begin to imagine being placed in prison for twenty years. You know that all of your life will change in that time; if you have family, and they stick by you, they too will have changed in ways you may not even recognise; the children will have grown up and left the nest ... You will want to escape, even if the chance to do so is negligible. But where to go? Even with money stashed away, who is prepared for this? *Are you?*

But it is no good us sentimentally thinking we can feel for the prisoner. Or even feeling sorry for them. Most criminals know the risks they take, know the punishments, know that, if they get recaptured, they're going to be beaten up and mistreated by the guards. Because they've been beaten for less in the past, particularly if they have a reputation as a hardman.

Today we read about the imprisonment and rape of Elisabeth Fritzl by her father in Austria, and think of the horror of twenty-four years underground, or of Natascha Kampusch, the Viennese schoolgirl who was kidnapped, aged ten, and held for eight years in her captor's garage before her escape. We think of the terror that they were submitted to, both physical and mental, but we barely equate any of that with being in one of society's prisons. For prisoners are there through some fault of their own, and, of course, some prisons are more lenient than others.

But any prison is a prison, though some are worse for all types of reasons – whether it is the physical conditions of the place, the level of restrictions, the management and officials who guard the inmates, or the brutality. For we cannot identify with the brutality as a whole, on every level, unless we have actually been there.

Prison Break

It should be pointed out that there is still some confusion over data with some cases, and, despite endless checking of conflicting reports, it is not always feasible to sort fact from fiction, truth from lies or fantasies. Indeed, some accounts have probably gone beyond the bounds of ever being resolved, as myths have become reality. In some places I've made the variations plain, and in at least one case I've made what left me incredulous read as incredible. But, generally, the other points don't affect the *modus operandi* of the escapes, which is the point of this book, after all.

No one side is ever correct when collecting information. The official versions from within the system are as capable (if not more so) of fudging, erasing or misleading as the criminals themselves. Each side has different things to hide at some time or another, or different individuals to protect.

But because testimony comes from the criminal side, that does not make it 'black' to the police's 'white'. How could it? (I was brought up in a house, where I am now sitting, not a stone's throw from the former home of a Flying Squad officer who was jailed for corruption in the 1970s.)

In prison there is often little to do but talk. So they tell each other stories, invent a little bit, or change the bits that weren't as good. And later, perhaps, they forget what is real and what is fabricated. It happens to everyone else, so why not to criminals? Why should all that you read here be the truth? Whose truth? The media's? Authors like me, who pen it? Or the villains who lived it, who may still wish to write down the truth but find that they can't? Somewhere amidst this sea of anecdotes there is a mass of exciting life stories … and many sad ones. But all these stories have been lived, and paid for, the hard way.

I concur with the French director Barbet Schroeder, who recently said of his film *Terror's Advocate*, "When I am doing a documentary I want the freedom of fiction. I cultivate everything that is fiction … People often think documentary is truth. Obviously, it is not. The minute you choose one shot instead of another you are entering fiction."

Despite the idea that to escape from prison is to leap into freedom, it is rarely forever. The more one reads of the cases, the more one knows that, even if the escape is meticulously planned and successfully carried out, the freedom gained may well be short … often only hours, if that. And one senses that the escapees know it too, even as they bid for their freedom. To escape brings with it all manner of problems; problems that may make many question the worth of such a tremendous effort. As is so often the case, one may well be replacing one prison with another, sometimes in the shape of one room, always watching one's back, fearing betrayal or worse. And yet to bid for that freedom, even with all its doubts, highlights how our very spirit and essence as human beings is otherwise at stake.

So what does one say to Walter Probyn, with his very singular attitude? "You don't need a lot of patience to plan an escape because you've got nothing else. Something like that is something to cherish while you've got it, it's a labour of love, something you really enjoy doing so you take your time doing it. It's like a hobby."

One final thought.

Throughout my research, I continually read of enormous leaps from one building's roof to another, or from one roof to another on a lower level. Having the opportunity to wander around a block of flats, I ventured onto building tops, estimating similar gaps, similar leaps … and wondered not only how brave, or how stupid, one would have to be to accomplish it, but how anyone could land without breaking bones, let alone twisting joints, even if that person was fit and knew how to roll on impact, assuming he cleared the distance in the first place.

Prison Break

Ankles broken, wrists sprained, backbones jarred, not only from leaps, but from drops over the walls – all these feature here, along with those who make it unscathed. Don't underestimate what is required to make those death-defying leaps across gaping spaces, or those heart-stopping drops down the sides of high walls.

I
Time to Go

As if the Great Train Robbery had not already gained its place in the annals of criminal history, usually with 'crime of the century' attached as an exhibit tag, the events that occurred after judicial proceedings finished lifted the offence onto a new level of notoriety.

One of these events is fitting to open these accounts, because it's not the norm for an inmate to escape prison via outsiders breaking in to swing open the cell door and indicate it's time to go. But that is what happened on 12 August 1964, when **Charlie Wilson**, one of the leaders of the Great Train Robbery, was freed from Winson Green Prison, a high-security jail near Birmingham. Wilson was barely four months into his thirty-year sentence.

Let us recapitulate and give context to this, the first of two audacious, high-profile escapes that would strike at the jugular of the penal system and reveal its laxity. Escapes which would elevate two of the robbers, Wilson and **Ronnie Biggs**, despite their opposing status within the robbery team, to a level that would reinforce the everlasting notoriety of the crime.

The Great Train Robbery occurred on the night of 8 August 1963. It netted £2,631,684 (equivalent to something in the region of £50 million or more, in today's terms) in used bank notes. The great British public, always on the lookout for entertaining newspaper stories through the summer holiday period, took to the escapade like a duck to water. Comedy films, in the manner of the *Carry On* series or *The Lavender Hill Mob*, were conjured up. These rascals had won the lottery, in today's terms, or the football pools in the vernacular of the day. Lucky blighters! But, as we all know, because the authorities made it abundantly clear, the train driver, Jack Mills, was coshed (though the robbers say punched) on the head. No one had suggested that violence should be treated lightly, but, as it seemed that the balance of public sympathy was tipping towards clemency for the villains, everyone had to pay. The public needed its wrists slapped, the criminals needed theirs cuffed. And to remain cuffed for a long time.

Whilst the accused were on remand awaiting trial, they knew that escape had to be urgently contemplated. For, though they were unaware of the hefty thirty-year sentences they would be receiving, they realised it would be easier to escape from the custody of their current residence than from any top-security prison they were to be carted off to after sentencing. The trial was not held in London, but in the area where the robbery occurred: Aylesbury, a market town in the county of Buckinghamshire. Thus the defendants were housed together in the hospital wing at Aylesbury Prison, which had been prepared especially for the occasion.

The initial plan of escape was to drug the two night guards, with Wilson doing the honours as it was his job each evening to prepare snacks and hot drinks in the small kitchen of the hospital wing. Once the guards were drugged, friends of the robbers would come over the wall and lead them out. Note that the inverse approach to escape was already under discussion. That possibility, however, was laid quickly to rest, once they discovered that drugging an officer was punishable by fourteen years' imprisonment.

Gordon Goody, another part of the robbery team's main force, had the job of cleaning the officers' quarters. He discovered that it was possible to enter the loft of the prison via a cupboard in one of their rooms, and from there to walk under the roof, right along to the end of the building, where one could remove some tiles and find a way down to the street below.

Their cells were locked at night from the outside, with one officer on guard in the corridor whilst another slept on the floor below. Goody set about making a key. He studied those hanging on the warder's chain, even asking if he could draw the guard – and his keys – whilst he was seated, playing chess with Biggs.

Overnight, he filed the necessary key from the appropriate blank with the needle files that had been brought in. The fit was successful. But, as the cell doors could only be opened from the outside, they needed help. Billy Boal had less secure confinement in a dormitory on the first floor, with a lock that could be easily removed with a chisel (also smuggled in). Boal was responsible for releasing Wilson and Goody. Then the pair of them would go down to the basement and take Biggs out of his cell. Only those three were determined to go at that point; the others had decided to remain, as they thought there was a reasonable chance that the charges wouldn't stick.

Wilson had arranged for his boys to have transport readied outside, behind the hospital. They had chosen a Saturday night as the traffic on the roads would be busier, making it easier to disappear.

However, on the scheduled evening Boal never showed. He appeared to have taken fright, worried that any appeal he might make sooner or later would have less chance of success, and his sentence might be increased when it was discovered he'd aided their breakout. This was relevant in his particular case, because Boal was not a train robber, or even a career criminal, but simply a friend of one of the robbers, Roger Cordrey, who'd unfortunately found himself in the wrong place at the wrong time.

The escape never happened, though the next morning the guards went straight to the crevices beneath the sinks in the washroom to find the key and the other equipment. They would likewise find further items in a ransacking of the cells. As always, this underlines how professionals throw a dice when they involve amateurs, no matter which *métier* we are talking about.

Charlie Wilson's next move back into the public eye occurred not long after, once he had received his thirty years. He had refused to attend his appeal against sentence, as he expected it would entail moving from Winson Green to a prison closer to the Appeals Court in London, where he would perhaps remain or be transferred to another prison altogether. He didn't want to move, for his escape plans were already underway. (Not that he told his lawyers; as far as they were concerned, his reason was that he didn't think he stood a chance on appeal.)

Nobody twigged that something was afoot. Even after it happened, there was a double-take on the fact that he had paid upfront for his daily newspaper to be delivered to his cell, right up to the end of that week. As if the cost of a few days' papers was important, when freedom was imminent.

Though many others shared three to a cell, Wilson merited a cell to himself. On maximum-security, he had to endure his light being kept on day and night, which meant he had to lessen its glare with black grease brought from the workshop. His prison employment entailed sewing mailbags which, given that he was incarcerated for robbing the Royal Mail, was a subject of some hilarity.

Prison Break

Wilson had been planning his escape right from the off. He'd sprinkled sugar on the floor outside his cell so that he could hear the warders patrolling at night, working out that it was at fifteen-minute intervals that they checked him through the spyhole in the door. He also noted that younger, tougher guards tended to be on duty at weekends. Given his high-risk status, he always had a warder with him, or close at hand, at all times of the day. As with so many of the people in this book, his chances of escape were limited, given the number of eyes watching over him – at least in theory.

Various accounts have been given as to how the escape was made. In essence, they all have the same *modus operandi*; only the perpetrators and what occurred beyond the prison walls seem to change.

It was just after 3am on Wednesday 12 August 1964 when Wilson's cell door in C-block was unlocked and three men in black stocking masks entered. Wilson was in his vest, his clothes being removed from the cell each night to hinder any escape attempt. He was tossed a bundle of clothes and hurriedly dressed in a black roll-neck sweater, dark trousers, plimsolls and a balaclava. They all walked down the corridor, passing the elderly guard who lay unconscious, having been coshed, bound and gagged, towards the centre of the prison and then through A-wing, passing the bathhouse before going down some stairs.

The intruder who had opened the locks of the various doors on the inward journey with duplicated keys systematically closed everything behind them. Indications of their entry and flight were thrown into disarray. Once outside, they kept to the shadows as the moon was bright, making for the twenty-foot walls. The three men who had entered to liberate Wilson were taking him back the same way as they came. They went up a rope ladder, dropping it, and then themselves, into a builder's yard next door, crossed another wall to a towpath beside a canal, and left in two cars that were waiting for them. It took little more than three minutes from leaving his cell for Wilson to land on *terra firma* outside the walls.

There are separate versions of events from here on. The first is that he was taken to a flat not far away, where they stayed for two days while arrangements were made by phone to move on the third day to a London safe house. Another account has it that they drove directly to London down the M1 and Wilson went to ground in a flat in Knightsbridge, where he remained for some months. His carer was not one of Wilson's known associates, which could be asking for trouble given the police pressure on his obvious contacts, but was connected to Charlie and Eddie Richardson. Many of the London villains didn't want to know where he was hiding, as it gave them "a kind of responsibility", as gang boss Joey Pyle later noted.

One of the more romantic escape stories that was spread around suggested that, once outside Winson Green, Wilson climbed into an adapted petrol tanker with two of his rescuers and reclined on mattresses whilst they were driven to a deserted airfield, from where he was flown to Northern France in a small plane.

Though the guard came round and was freed by 3:20am, reporting the escape to the orderly officer, they didn't report it for a further thirty minutes as they believed the intruders were still in the building and might attack them. The other guard on C-block had actually gone down to the kitchens to start cooking the breakfast porridge, leaving the five night staff who patrolled all the wings effectively locked in without a pass key.

The police were roused, not through any emergency system but via a direct call at 3:50am. They arrived at 4am and had to wait at the main gate until someone with keys could let them in. By then Wilson was well away. It was a few hours before a full alert was in operation and the traffic scrutinised.

Prison Break

Wilson's copy of the *Daily Sketch*, with the photos and story of his breakout splashed across the front page, was delivered to his empty cell the following day.

On the other side of the world, Bruce Reynolds, the leader of the Great Train Robbers, still not arrested at that point, said that when he saw the headlines, "His success filled me with pride. We'd finessed the Establishment yet again."

Charlie Wilson had taken leave of prison life not by breaking out, but by others breaking in to open his cell door. This seemed to be a first, at least in modern times. Once again, the whole world was laughing. No one knew precisely how they had obtained duplicates of the keys, other than through a corrupt officer at the prison. Only half a dozen master keys existed and they were closely guarded. It was said that traces of soap were found on one, signifying that a copy had been made from an impression in a bar of soap, though other reports claim this wasn't so.

The escape had hit a sore point, and the police search for Wilson was not going to die down quickly. He grew a beard and, by the end of the year, realised his only way to regain anything akin to a normal life was to go abroad. In March 1965 he left from Dover, catching a channel ferry to Calais, masquerading as a schoolteacher on a hitchhiking holiday. He was collected by car in the French port and driven to the South of France where, a couple of months later, his wife and one of his daughters joined him in a villa at Ramatuelle, near St Tropez. That was to be the start of his foreign adventures, until his capture in Rigaud, a suburb of Montréal, just under three and a half years later by the Royal Canadian Mounted Police.

After he had finally served his sentence, Wilson moved with his wife to a town near Marbella in Spain. He died bloodily in 1990, gunned down by a young visitor sent to assassinate him. Not long after, the drug dealer who is believed to have issued the contract was himself shot down, in a bar in Amsterdam.

The idea that others should come into a prison to collect an inmate resonates with earlier times, as we will note with the cases of **Jack Sheppard** and **Bonnie and Clyde**, both from different eras. Our notions of the American Wild West, as seen in countless films, include the associates of jailed men marching into the sheriff's office with guns drawn to rescue them from their cells. Even the **John Dillinger** story has an angle on this method.

In modern times, such approaches have to be a bit more sophisticated. With that said, going over a wall *into* a prison is not an unheard of event. There are stories of people going over to leave tools hidden in the prison yard for their friends inside to collect, or to deliver drugs. There are recent accounts of prisoners going out for a 'pub crawl' and then climbing back in to sleep it off, or, in one case, of a prisoner getting so drunk that he couldn't manage to get his leg back over the wall. There are even stories of burglars scaling the wall into Brixton Prison to raid the staff officers' club – more than once! A further twist will appear later, when we look at the notorious French criminal and escapee **Pascal Payet** …

II
Going Places

It is only to be expected that our gadget-laden world will provide ever more powerful and sophisticated surveillance cameras to maintain watch over those imprisoned – along with superior designs of locks and other fastening contrivances that make it difficult for duplicate keys to open them. And that's not to forget sensors that can pick up slight vibrations, ideal for use at night.

The job of the escapee is rarely an easy one, particularly for those in the most secure prisons, or 'prisons within prisons', as some are now styled. But it has always been the case that a prisoner in transit is passing through the penal system's weakest link, whether being taken to prison in the first instance, transferred from one prison to another, or transported to court for an appearance. The prison system itself inadvertently presents this enticement via its own policy of unsettling prisoners by continually shifting them from one prison to another, providing greater potential for escape than is perhaps necessary. Of course, there are also instances when prisoners themselves engineer a day out in court just to take advantage of that weakest link, making a bid for freedom in the most fundamental way.

Such an occasion attracted attention in May 1966, at the time of a spate of escapes. The government of the day ordered a report by Earl Mountbatten into what it saw as an intolerable situation, which recommended a mass of improvements to prison security. The escape in question was hatched in Parkhurst Prison on the Isle of Wight by **John McVicar**, whom we will encounter again in his role in another major breakout. The Parkhurst inmates knew that if they caused an incident (in this case one prisoner stabbing another), it would require them being taken before Winchester Assizes on the mainland.

This is indeed what happened, and on return from their day out, thirteen convicts (nine of whom were involved in the plot) set about seven prison officers and escaped. The authorities had received a tip-off that an attempt would occur, but the likelihood pointed to it happening at Portsmouth, where they would take the ferry back to the island. Police had been deployed around the terminal for just such an eventuality but they had it wrong, for it happened as the coach passed through Bishop's Waltham.

The prisoners had three improvised keys with them. Ten of the men who had been handcuffed in pairs freed themselves. The other three were joined to prison officers. On a signal, the freed men jumped up, most going for the guards whilst another went for the driver to take control of the steering wheel. As the coach ground to a halt, the door was opened and nine men took off.

The police escort behind them radioed for help, and two policemen quickly multiplied to one hundred and twenty personnel, along with dogs and an RAF helicopter. Seven prisoners were rounded up within a few hours, and another one a couple of days later. Only two got clean away, McVicar being one of them. He had all summer to stretch his legs before being recaptured.

And yet, despite such machinations, there will always be room for the opportunist to seize the moment. John Bindon, the villain-turned-actor (*Poor Cow*, *Get Carter*, *Performance*), who helped give the 'hardman' archetype its cinematic image in 1970s Britain, recounted how, in his earlier days, he was being transferred by prison bus from one borstal to another, along with his friend **Alan Stanton**.

It appears that Stanton had small wrists and was able to slip out of his handcuffs, and from there to abscond out of the window. No other details are given, other than it was in "the middle of London". All we know is that Stanton immediately stole a car, for he is reputed to have driven past the prison bus, catching the eye of Bindon, still seated at his window. When the officers asked where "the little one" had gone, Bindon informed them he had just waved at him from a passing car.

Stanton wasn't the first to thumb his nose in such a humorous way. It is recorded that, two and a half centuries earlier, after escaping from Newgate Prison, **Jack Sheppard** rode past the gates of that same prison in a carriage with a woman on either side, all of them the worse for drink, only to end the night recaptured. He was subsequently hanged at Tyburn shortly after. (Things were not quite so drastic for Stanton, though he was caught within two weeks.)

In the century after Sheppard, that habitual prisoner, **Charles Peace**, the original 'old lag', having committed countless thefts, burglaries and two murders, thought to hurl himself out of the window of a moving train. He was being taken from London's King's Cross (starting the day at Pentonville Prison, where he was serving life for the attempted murder of a policeman) north to Sheffield, to stand trial for murder. He had originally been taken up on 17 January 1879, to be charged before the stipendiary magistrate, and was returned to London until the second hearing on the 22nd. Again they took the early morning train to Sheffield at 5:15am. We are not talking Eurostar or high-speed trains, but they still sped along at a fair rate, and the reality of clambering out must have been more hazardous than some James Bond fantasy. In fact, Peace hurt himself on landing and was recaptured.

Peace had not initially intended to leap when it was moving. At any station where the train stopped, he tried to find excuses to go down to the toilet. He had probably tried this on the earlier trip, for the two warders had provided bags for him to use – and then throw out of the window! Peace used the act of disposal as his excuse for opening the window, and made his bid for freedom by taking a flying leap through it. One warder caught his left foot just in time. Peace held onto the footboard and kicked furiously with his right to free himself. The other warder, unable to get to the window, pulled on the communication cord to urge the driver to stop. The train steamed on for a mile, with Peace desperate to liberate his foot. When he finally freed it from his shoe and tumbled down onto the line, it still took another mile before the driver halted the train, and only then due to encouragement from passengers in other carriages.

Though the warders ran back along the line ahead of the reversing train, they needn't have worried. Peace was still lying beside the track, near Kiveton Park, unconscious and bleeding from a bad wound on his head. He was lifted back into the guard's van of the train and taken to the police station at Sheffield, where he was attended by a surgeon. The case was adjourned for eight days.

The method works much better if one can get the means of transport to slow down considerably – particularly if it's an airplane. This is supposedly the case with **Frank Abagnale**. For a few years, starting in his late teens, he led a busy and successful life as a confidence trickster, forger and impostor, details of which were recorded in a book that reads like a Steven Spielberg movie. (Which in fact is what it became. Called *Catch Me If You Can*, it starred Leonardo DiCaprio as Abagnale.)

Abagnale's personal adventures offer an impressive escape from a plane, a British Viscount VC-10, flying him back to face trial and undoubted imprisonment in the United States in 1971. Excusing himself to go to the toilet, just before the pilot signalled to fasten seatbelts, Abagnale released the toilet fasteners from its apparatus, a self-contained unit, and climbed down into the space beneath, knowing there was a hatch used to remove the in-flight toilet waste at the end of each journey. After the plane landed on Runway 13 at JFK International Airport, he waited for the moment it slowed, and then virtually stopped, as it turned to the taxi strip. Then he dropped ten feet from the hatch to the ground and made his getaway, leaving the FBI agents on the plane staring at an empty toilet. It begs the question of how he managed to stay in the toilet once the crew knew he was not fastened in his seat, but no one seems to have checked out his disappearance at that point.

Abagnale scaled a cyclone fence under cover of darkness, took a cab to Grand Central Station, then a train to the Bronx to visit a girl who had stashed some clothes, money and a set of keys for a Montréal safe deposit box for him. Leaving her most of the money, he took a train for Montréal. There he collected $20,000 and proceeded to Dorval Airport to take a flight to São Paulo, knowing that the United States had no extradition treaty with Brazil. But he never made the flight, for a Royal Canadian Mounted Policeman saw him in line at the ticket counter. He was later escorted to the Canadian border and handed over to the US Border Patrol. Today, Frank Abagnale runs a financial fraud consultancy company, and can be viewed on YouTube talking about his exploits.

It's not impossible to escape from a moving plane (on the ground, anyway). It happened in California in December 1985, when **Reginald Still** was being taken to Sacramento to stand trial. No sooner had the plane landed, and slowed to around fifty miles per hour, than Still broke open the emergency door and leapt onto the wing, then the runway, leaving eight guards behind on the plane. And he was wearing leg irons and handcuffs at the time!

In much the same way, **Mickey Green**, a.k.a. 'the Pimpernel' (a name acquired by evading arrest for more than twenty years), a successful armed robber in the 1970s before moving on to the lucrative ventures of gold bullion and drug smuggling, took the opportunity to escape from the airport itself, en route from California to Paris. FBI agents had arrested him in 1993, at the former mansion home of Rod Stewart that he was renting in Beverly Hills. As he was wanted in Paris to serve seventeen years for a drug trafficking conviction, he was being flown back across the Atlantic. Though Green had British nationality, he also carried an Irish passport. When the plane made a stopover at Shannon Airport, he simply alighted from the plane and slipped through customs. As extradition terms between Ireland and France were weak at the time, he decided to stay in Dublin for a while, acquiring a luxurious property outside the capital. Later he moved on to Spain, when his presence came to the attention of the IRA and he was advised that he might do well to depart.

What is quite remarkable is how so-called dangerous men who are facing heavy sentences are sometimes moved around in such cavalier ways. School kids are used to the hired coach for their days out breaking down en route, as schools cut corners on the financial outlay. But it seems the prison authorities have no more foresight.

In November 1996, Blundeston Prison in Suffolk needed to transfer ten prisoners to Wandsworth Prison in London. But they had no vehicle available, so they hired a private coach with its driver. It barely moved two miles down the road before it broke down, and a replacement had to be sent along so that six of the ten could continue on their journey. The six, five of whom were robbers – **Lee**

Mitty, **Warren Edwards**, **Gary Staggs**, **Christopher Ward** and **David Currey** – and the other, **Stewart Warwick**, jailed for possession of firearms, were only accompanied by five officers, whereas it would be usual to have a dozen for six prisoners in transit, particularly as they were regarded as dangerous, and three of them (Mitty, Edwards and Staggs) had impressive records for escape. Not that the prison officers knew of their records; perhaps they did not even know they were being moved because they had formed a gang inside the prison, and had been involved in a fight resulting in some unpleasant injuries. As was noted by a perplexed Prison Officers Association representative, "It is very strange that they [the prison service] were trying to split up the gang by taking them from a secure environment on to a standard coach." And all together, at the same time too.

When they were going down the M25 it appeared that the prisoners slipped their handcuffs, one of them showing the others how to dislocate the thumb to achieve this. Around the Waltham Abbey area of Essex, they took over the coach and viciously set about the officers, inflicting quite extensive bodily damage with the captured truncheons. They also destroyed all their personal files, which were travelling with them, hurling the ripped documents out of the window, and changed into their civilian clothes which were also on board. In the meantime, the coach driver was forced to press on with his journey towards the capital. When they reached Duncombe Road in Archway, their ride over, they all climbed down and escaped.

Similarly, in February 1992, **John McFayden**, who was two years into a life sentence for murder, in addition to forty-seven years for drug offences, was being taken by taxi from Full Sutton, near York, down to Wormwood Scrubs in London, apparently to see relatives, when he pulled a blade on the two-man escort and ordered the female taxi driver to drive him to Euston. Though he was caught before the year was out, it still seems remarkable that pre-travel body searches can be so sloppily carried out, particularly for such a vulnerable transportation system which, as the Home Office pointed out, was used dozens of times each day.

In the course of his reminiscences, the late Reggie Kray mentions the escapes of a few men he met inside. One can't fail to notice the role that 'pulling a blade' plays in these actions. He notes how **Steve McFadden** escaped in transit from one prison to another, producing a knife and injuring one of his four escorts in his bid for freedom. Another friend of his, **Micky Fenlon**, pulled one of these prison-crafted knives on his way to Exeter Prison, hijacking the coach with all its occupants, convicts and officers. The vehicle was driven someway towards London before he parted company and made his own way.

A nightmare situation presents itself in the case of **Billy Hughes**, who was to all appearances a petty criminal who had served five sentences for housebreaking, before being charged with rape and grievous bodily harm. He was held on remand in Leicester Prison, where it appears that his criminal record was slow in catching up with him. In fact, it was at the prison but not delivered to the appropriate department until the day after he escaped. The man the warders thought was a pleasant character had a history of violence against the police that included killing two police dogs with his bare hands. He was not really the ideal person to place in the prison kitchen, where he spirited away a seven-inch boning knife six weeks before using it. (No search was made by the authorities despite the knife going missing.)

And if they had been more competent, they might have thought better of taking him to Chesterfield Magistrates' Court for his weekly remand appearances by taxi, accompanied by two not particularly tough officers. Or indeed, they might have searched him thoroughly and not casually frisked him. Hughes managed to prolong the court procedures for ten trips by giving contradictory instructions to his solicitors, requiring further days out. All the time he was preparing for his escape.

Hughes struck on 12 January 1977, as the hire car turned off the M1 at Junction 29. There he leaned forward and dealt the warder in the front-passenger seat a blow to his head. Then he turned to the officer he was handcuffed to in the backseat, produced the boning knife and slashed him across the neck, causing a deep five-inch wound. As the warder in front recovered and turned, Hughes lunged at him with the knife, making two vicious strokes, one slashing his hand, the other exposing his jawbone.

Hughes ordered the car to go straight through Chesterfield and out onto the moors. At Stonedge he stopped the car, had his handcuffs unlocked and pushed everyone out to the side of the road, cuffed them together and collected whatever money they had between them. Then he jumped back in the car and fled. It was a cold, snowy January and the roads were bleak. He lost control on the ice within two miles and crashed into a wall at Beeley, near Chatsworth, home of the Duke of Devonshire. Once the alarm was raised by the warders, warnings were issued quickly to all within the area and roadblocks were set up.

An extensive search of farmhouses and local properties was made. Police guards were placed on his most recent lover in Chesterfield, as she had told him they were finished whilst he was on remand. Police also expected he might return to Blackpool, where his estranged wife had earlier received death threats from him.

For some reason, Billy Hughes was missed by all those searching for him. He had gone to ground less than a mile from the place where he was last sighted, not long after he hijacked the taxi –

Pottery Cottage in the hamlet of Eastmoor, close to the headquarters set up by the police at the local pub, the Highwayman.

Pottery Cottage was to become a scene of carnage. On his arrival Hughes had taken hostage an elderly couple he found there, Arthur and Amy Minton. Later, as other members of the family arrived home, Gill and Richard Moran, and their ten-year-old daughter Sarah, were also taken and locked in separate rooms. Though he killed Sarah and her grandfather, Arthur, immediately, he still kept the survivors separate and maintained the pretence that each was alive by taking food into their rooms at mealtimes.

The next day council workers came to clean the septic tank, as Sarah's mother drove alone to fetch a newspaper and cigarettes for Hughes. No outsider had any inkling that something was wrong and she gave no sign that Hughes was in her home. Later that day, Hughes went out with Gill on errands. Each time nothing untoward occurred. The following day, Richard and Gill went shopping and filled the car with petrol. A while later, Hughes and the husband went to the plastics company where Moran worked and stole £200 from the safe.

That evening the grandmother, Amy, tried to escape through a window. Hughes caught her, slit her throat, and left her in the garden covered in snow. It was time for him to depart. The only two members of the family still alive were the husband and wife, though they remained in the dark as to the fate of their loved ones.

Hughes decided to take only Gill with him, and tied up her husband back at the house. However, the tyres of the family's Chrysler car would not grip in the snow, so they knocked on a neighbour's door and asked to be towed out. Ready to depart, Hughes returned to the house and stabbed the husband to death.

What he did not know was that Gill had whispered to the neighbour about her predicament, and the police were about to join their trail. Soon in attendance at the cottage, they would realise the gravity of the situation.

Having chosen such bad weather for his escape, any form of car chase was doomed to end in a further crash. When this happened Hughes kept Gill Moran as his hostage, his knife at her throat. Switching to one of the police cars, a fresh chase got underway that led into Cheshire and a further crash into a bus that was used as a roadblock. With the woman as his hostage, he demanded another car.

In the meantime, police marksmen had arrived. When an outside light at a nearby house came on suddenly, it triggered a dramatic *mêlée* as Hughes started swinging an axe he had brought along, both at his hostage and the police, who were trying to get into the car. One marksman shot him in the head from twelve feet through the windscreen, with a Smith & Wesson .38. Another shot forced Hughes to try to clamber from the car, at which point he was shot in the chest. In the first such incident in modern times, the British police had shot dead a prison escapee.

Some people leave it right to the last minute until their bid to escape is put into operation. The escape of **Clifford Hobbs** and **Noel Cunningham** took place in June 2003. As the Securicor van taking ten remand prisoners from Brixton Prison to the Inner London Crown Court turned into Avonmouth Street, just along from the Elephant and Castle, it halted outside the gate to the court's yard and waited to be admitted. It was just after 9am. Two men who had been seen loitering earlier in the nearby park stepped in front of the van. One was dressed as a postman and carried a Royal Mail bag. Both were armed with handguns.

The 'postman' demanded that the driver open the hatches. The driver wasn't successful so he was told to open the side door. He was then shot in the knee. The second gunman ordered the emergency hatches (used in the event of a serious accident) to be released. Then the two men entered the van, and the prison escort was made to unlock the door to the separate cells after being pistol-whipped. The rear doors were then opened for the prisoners to escape, none of whom were handcuffed. All ten were given the opportunity to run, but only three escaped – though one, Tony Peters, surrendered later that same day.

The breakout had been organised for Hobbs and Cunningham. They were due in court to face charges of conspiracy to steal £1.25 million from a Securicor van in Effra Road, Brixton, a robbery that failed when they were ambushed by the Flying Squad. Once out of the van, they and their liberators ran across the nearby park, Newington Gardens, before going their separate ways, one in a getaway car from Bath Terrace, the other on the back of a motorbike from Brockham Street.

Four years later in court, Hobbs denied that the breakout was planned and claimed he had simply taken advantage of the opportunity when it presented itself. Conflictingly, the court was told how he indicated his whereabouts in the van by tapping on the window. Hobbs is known to have lain low for a few days in south London before obtaining a false passport and fleeing to Spain. He was tracked down and arrested at Puerto Banus, near Malaga, in August 2007. For some while it had been bandied about that he was a prime suspect in the £53 million Securitas heist in Tonbridge, in February 2006, but this seems to be unfounded. Noel Cunningham has not been recaptured, but is believed by some to be on the 'Costa del Crime'.

In September 1984, **Terry Smith** and **John Kendall** were moved to Maidstone Prison in Kent, ostensibly to further their educational studies, though they planned to go over the wall. Things changed, and the pair of them, both armed robbers, were marked for transfer back to Parkhurst Prison on the Isle of Wight at the earliest opportunity. Smith was still determined to escape and informed his friend outside, Tommy Hole, that he was moving the following week, on 20 November. He told no one inside the prison, not even Kendall.

Kendall undoubtedly sensed something was going down, because he asked Smith on the morning of the transfer and was told that something might happen. If they were cuffed together, he should just hold his arms out "and they will be bolt-cropped." Kendall was cuffed to Smith, and the other prisoner on the ride, a Turkish inmate, was joined to an officer. The officer in charge sat in the front of a yellow Bedford minibus with bars on the windows, alongside the driver, whilst three other officers sat in the back with the prisoners.

No sooner had they left the prison than the van stopped at a newsagent's, for the senior officer to rush in to buy a paper. Smith noticed a BMW pull in front of them and one of its occupants go into the shop. As the man came out he looked directly at Smith in the van. Smith told me recently that he was thinking, "What's he come in his own car for?"

"I was worried that they had just come down to see if it was genuine I was leaving," rather than to implement the escape. But, whatever was going to happen now, he had to wait. He was entirely in their hands.

The prison van joined the M20 heading for the M25 link someway up the road. They were followed at a respectable distance by two BMW's. As their occupants were all professional criminals, they knew how to tail a van without being spotted. (Don't believe movies or TV crime programmes where everyone hangs so close together that only an idiot wouldn't rumble it.) As Smith recalls, "It was a *bright* yellow van. When you're doing the visuals you can hang back a good two miles and stay out of sight. On a motorway it's perfect. And they want to get onto those motorways as soon as they can."

An hour after leaving Maidstone, when the van was turning off the M25 to go south on the A217 to Reigate at Junction 8, one of the BMW's appeared, shot past the van and smashed into the driver's side, forcing the vehicle off the road and onto the grass verge. At the same time the second BMW blocked the van from behind. Two masked men leapt from the first BMW; one, wielding a pickaxe handle, smashed the windscreen whilst the other, carrying bolt croppers, grabbed the van's keys and headed for the rear doors.

Smith leapt forward onto the officer in the passenger seat, thrashing to free himself as he was rugby-tackled from behind. Wary of the 'outside help', the senior officer instructed his staff to let them go. Smith dragged Kendall out with him through the passenger side and into the back of the waiting BMW, whilst the rescuer who had wrenched open the back door found Smith and Kendall were already going out the front way. Making a U-turn the BMW sped back past the van and the traffic building up at the scene, shot over the elevated roundabout and down a string of country lanes until it was time to split up and go their separate ways. Smith took one of his associates, his friend Tommy Hole, along with Kendall onto a commuter train at Coulsdon, bound for Victoria, whilst his other two friends found a different route home.

It was close to twenty months before Smith and Kendall were recaptured, after a robbery that went disastrously wrong for Smith, who seriously injured his leg and was lucky not to lose it altogether.

Sheer force was the method of armed robber **Vic Dark** in September 1988, when he was being taken across London from Hackney police station to Wormwood Scrubs Prison. They had handcuffed him, daisy-chain fashion, with two sets of cuffs to the bars of the window. They had secured him so well that he wasn't expected to be any trouble. But Dark wanted out and knew he would have "to Rambo it", as he said later. There was no other way than to rip the whole window grille away from the bodywork of the Ford Transit van.

The bars came away, leaving him handcuffed but able to manoeuvre. He kicked out the window itself and was halfway through before the officer in the front seat reacted and grabbed his legs. In the meantime, the other guard had pulled the van up in the Gray's Inn Road and gone around the outside to prevent him coming out of the window. Extra help arrived, and the four-strong team moved into the back to watch over Dark, taking him back to Hackney to start the whole process of transfer over again. If he had levered himself out he would have landed on his head, like poor Charlie Peace. But at least his transport would have been brought to a halt.

One of the most notorious escapees in the United States through the 1920s was **Roy Gardner.** His exploits could have filled a book – which indeed he could have written, for he was an educated man, had taught in the English department at a Midwestern college and wasn't slow to flaunt his knowledge, once making Shakespearian references to a judge in court. In his early days he had become a gunrunner during the Mexican Revolution, and, though he was arrested, he escaped the firing squad and returned to the States, where he became a prize-fighter and sparring partner to heavyweight champion J. J. Jeffries at his training camp in Reno, Nevada, during the summer of 1910.

Though he had an extensive criminal record which included escapes, Gardner was stunned by what he saw as the inappropriateness of a twenty-five-year sentence at McNeil Island Federal Penitentiary, Washington, for robbing the US Mail. His response to the judge was, "You'll never get me there." He wasn't joking. On the train journey to prison in June 1920, he distracted the two marshals escorting him by drawing their attention to something out of the window, and then reached for one of their guns, overpowered them, and fled near Portland, Oregon.

It wasn't long before he was caught again, being a basically unsuccessful criminal. After receiving another twenty-five years for armed train robbery, he was once more placed on a train bound for McNeil Island. And once again they failed to get him there, just as he had warned them. (The papers had printed his boast.) On board the train he asked to go to the toilet. The officers went with him, and took along another prisoner, **Norris Pryor**, handcuffing both men together. All four fitted into a toilet cubicle that was obviously built larger back in those days. After relieving himself, Gardner moved to the sink to complete his ablutions, but instead slipped his hand under and withdrew a gun – no one knows how it was placed there, as he was very much a lone criminal. Gardner and Pryor handcuffed the officers together, bound their mouths with the tape used to secure the gun beneath the sink, and alighted from the train in the Vancouver yards, disappearing into a misty rain. With the major press coverage his escape received, it was inevitable that Gardner was soon recaptured and transported in a more security-conscious manner to prison.

To conclude his story, it wasn't long before Gardner determined that prison was still not for him. After little more than six weeks, whilst watching a baseball game on the prison field, he slipped beneath the bleacher seats to the ground below with two others, when the attention of inmates and guards was absorbed by a big hit in the opposite direction. With wire cutters he had brought along from the machine shop, Gardner breached the fence.

There was an expanse of open space ahead that had to be covered before undergrowth and trees would provide relative cover. Halfway across, the tower guards saw the escapees and opened fire. Both his friends were halted in their tracks, but Gardner, though hit in the leg, dragged himself onward to the bushes. Extensive searches were made and security craft circled the island, but he could not be found.

They didn't know he had returned to the prison and was hiding in the barn, nourishing himself by milking a cow, and tending to his wound. After forty-eight hours the search was called off, the guards suspecting he had reached the mainland. Few had managed it before, for the island was surrounded by ice-cold water and fast currents. But Gardner set off from the prison again, made it to the water and drifted two and a half miles to Fox Island, from whence he swam to the mainland. That was to be his last escape. When he was recaptured he served all of his sentence, all further attempts at tunnelling under the wall, sawing through bars or taking hostages ending in failure.

If we return to earlier times for a perspective on today's escapes in transit, we find that in 1831, **Ikey Solomons** (on whom Charles Dickens probably based Fagin in *Oliver Twist*), whilst in Newgate Prison facing a charge of receiving stolen goods, applied for a writ of habeas corpus so that he might be released on bail. He never expected it to be successful, but it would mean a visit to court.

Solomons was taken there in a coach by two Newgate turnkeys. Whilst waiting to be called, he suggested he take the officers to a public house to 'refresh' them. When they returned to the court, Solomons' application was dismissed and he was escorted back to the coach to return to Newgate. En route, he convinced his guards to stop off for more refreshments at another pub. Resuming their journey, they were joined by Mrs Solomons, who climbed into the carriage and promptly threw a fit. Solomons suggested they make a detour down Petticoat Lane and drop his wife off at a friend's home. One guard was "stupidly drunk" and the other wanted shot of the woman, so the idea was agreed upon. Surprisingly, on arrival at the address, Mrs Solomons stepped down, quickly followed by her husband, dashed into the house and locked the door behind them.

Ikey Solomons was not recaptured until many years later ... in Australia.

III
Under Your Noses

Films and television series like to show the criminal leaping spectacularly to freedom through the courtroom window, no sooner than sentence has been pronounced. Right before the judge and jury, with two fingers in the air to all and sundry; it looks thrilling. Yet open windows do not necessarily equate with an easy escape. Who's to know where the police or other guards happen to be situated around the premises? For the escapee it's a calculated gamble. Nevertheless, it still happens.

It seems that **Albert Spaggiari** had it all worked out for his appearance before the examining magistrate in Nice, where he was accused of masterminding the famous robbery of the safe deposit boxes at the Société Générale bank. His team had tunnelled into the vaults from the sewer system and had spent the weekend systematically rifling the boxes, taking cash, gold, gems and jewellery estimated at sixty million francs – according to the insurance claims made afterwards, though many believe that was only a fraction of the undeclared items such boxes contain. And even then they only opened three hundred and seventeen out of four thousand boxes, their haul curtailed by a storm that triggered the sewer system back into action.

Given that Spaggiari was a photographer and had been arrested on his return from a visit to the Far East as official photographer of the Mayor of Nice, Jacques Médecin, perhaps it's not surprising that he left behind in the plundered vault an exhibition of sexually compromising photos discovered in the boxes of wealthy local dignitaries. Presumably he hoped to give the scene-of-crime team and local media something to get their teeth into. Out of the twenty-six-strong gang, only Spaggiari and six others were rounded up, thanks to a tip-off from someone's ex-girlfriend.

On 10 March 1977, Spaggiari created a distraction to cover his escape from the magistrate's office. He presented a document to the magistrate to examine before turning to the window, complaining of the heat, opening it and leaping through, falling nine feet onto the roof of a parked car and escaping on the back of a waiting motorcycle. The car owner later claimed he had received a cheque in the post to pay for the damage. This seemed consistent with the man who had scrawled on a wall in the bank vault, "Without hatred, without violence, without guns."

Spaggiari was never caught. He probably spent most of the next twelve years until his death in Argentina, though it was believed he slipped in and out of France regularly. He could certainly afford to.

Jacques Mesrine was France's most famous robber through the 1960's and 70's, a reputation enhanced by the nature of his escapes. His first on home soil was from a court in 1973, when he took the judge hostage. Mesrine had earlier visited the court with his associates to show them around, and to determine where guns should be planted if he were brought to trial. He was carrying out so many robberies by then that it was inevitable. But he knew that, once they started to draw up charges against him, they would have to take them in chronological order, which would mean commencing with the relatively minor crime of passing dud cheques some years earlier. Any trial would be held at Compiègne, the nearest town with a court.

He was right. On 6 June 1973 he was taken by train from Paris to Compiègne, fifty miles away. The carriage had been reserved for Mesrine and his entourage of armed guards. Mesrine was to maintain a theme throughout the day of having a bad stomach, "attacks of dysentery" as he called them. He regularly requested the toilet and on each visit a guard would check out the cubicle first, in case anyone had hidden a weapon there. He went three times on the hour-long train journey. On arrival at the station, the local police joined the escort as he was loaded into a police van – though not before he noticed one of his accomplices in the forecourt flick a cigarette to the ground, the sign that all was going as planned.

Mesrine was taken to the police station and placed in a cell, though regular visits to the toilet were carried out to maintain his ruse. The court session was scheduled for after lunch and he relaxed with his escort on the drive there, lulling them into a false sense of security. As they pulled into the Palais de Justice courtyard, Mesrine saw his accomplice outside in the street, behind the wheel of a white Alfa Romeo.

Whilst waiting to be called into court, he asked for the toilet again and was led, still handcuffed, to the outside public conveniences. After it was checked he entered the first cubicle and complained that there was no toilet paper. They tried the second, which was "filthy", and he demanded to be taken back inside. The guard suggested they try the lawyers' toilet upstairs. This time, as Mesrine expected, the guard did not check first, and, though still handcuffed to his escort, he managed to withdraw a 9mm Luger from behind the cistern and stick it in his belt. His forward thinking some months earlier had paid off.

Back outside the courtroom, Mesrine waited on the bench. When he was called, he asked if his handcuffs could be unlocked. They refused and he remained attached to one of his guards as he entered the court. No sooner had Monsieur Guérin, the presiding judge, started to read the charge than Mesrine leapt forward, dragging the guard with him, and grabbed the judge, threatening to kill him as he waved his Luger with the other hand. Mesrine ordered his cuffs to be unlocked, then, with everyone in the court forced to lie on the floor, he dragged the judge as his shield towards the door, firing a couple of shots into the courtroom to show that he meant business. Out of the court, he kept moving towards the gates, whilst policemen moved towards him with raised guns, too scared to shoot for fear of hitting the judge.

As Mesrine made the street, he pushed the judge aside and sprinted the hundred yards to the getaway car. Bullets sped past him, one hitting his right arm. As he reached the Alfa Romeo, the door opened and he leapt in. They pulled out as a police van drove straight into their path. Mesrine's driver reversed and swung round before the police driver could react. As they swerved past Mesrine fired through the van's windscreen, hitting its driver.

Mesrine had made a thorough reconnaissance earlier and planned the best way out, using minor roads because, as expected, roadblocks had been erected on the main roads. Twenty miles away, at Meaux, they switched cars to reach a farm hideout. They had covered all eventualities, including a shootout, and first aid was available to remove his bullet. What particularly pleased Mesrine that night, as he celebrated, was that when he was arrested he had boasted to the Commissaire that he would escape within three months. He had done just that, by two days.

Prison Break

This is an appropriate place to give **Alfred Hinds** his first outing in this book. Hinds was in full battle with the justice system, to the extent of conducting his own defence. He made escapes to publicise his claim that he was fitted-up over a jewel robbery at the Maples department store in London. He was frustrated by the way the system continually misread the way he interpreted the law books that he now buried himself in. These legal points might have been of little consequence to many in the judicial system, for they received their wages and went home at the end of each day, their battles seemingly little more than intellectual games. For Hinds, it was his freedom that was at stake. It was *not* a game.

Hinds had determined that, during his next trip to the Law Courts in the Strand, he was going to make another escape bid. (As we will see later, he had previously made a famous escape from Nottingham Prison in November 1955, with Patsy Fleming.) Upon arrival at the Law Courts from Pentonville Prison, on 25 June 1957, his handcuffs were removed and he led the officers to the staff canteen for tea and coffee. Hinds found a padlock and key taped, as arranged, under a canteen table. He had expected only a key, but would find out why soon enough.

Moving up to the courtroom, Hinds reminded his two guards it was advisable to go to the toilet prior to stepping into court. The key his friend had provided would fit the toilet door. As he approached, he saw two "of the biggest and brightest" nickel-plated screw eyes, one on the jamb, the other on the door. "They were like searchlights." Now he knew why he had been passed the padlock. He opened the toilet door for the officers and ushered them in before him, as he had done at every door since they had arrived at the court. They went through. Hinds grabbed the door and pulled it shut after them, whipped the padlock out and fastened it through the eyes. His guards were imprisoned in the toilet.

Hinds became lost among the crowds and activity of the courts. As he made his way out into Bell Yard, he saw his wife, Peg, and made himself known as he hurried past. He slipped across the Strand and down a turning for Temple tube station. His brother Bert, who had seen his escape, caught up and arranged to meet him at Waterloo station in thirty minutes.

Bert arrived with a car, driven by a friend, and took Hinds to London Airport. The Dublin flight had just left, so they raced for Bristol to catch a flight there. By an unlucky chance, Bert made himself suspicious to the girl at the desk as he bought his brother's ticket. She called the police, believing he might be connected with a local murder enquiry. All three were arrested. The clerk said later that if she'd known it was Alfie Hinds she wouldn't have called the police, such was the feeling among many people in England about the press coverage of his case.

Most guards (like most people) have an unwarranted sense of trust and decency in allowing a person some privacy in places like the toilet. The infamous serial killer, **Ted Bundy**, even managed to exploit that trust in being allowed to use the law library on his own.

Bundy had initially been arrested in August 1975, in Salt Lake City, on suspicion of burglary. A search of his apartment led to evidence that was to convict him of the kidnap of Carol DaRonch, for which he was given fifteen years in Utah State Prison. As the Colorado authorities were pursuing a murder charge against him in relation to the death of Caryn Campbell, they asked for him to be transferred there in January 1977.

On 7 June Bundy was taken to the Pitkin County courthouse in Aspern, in preparation for another hearing for his murder trial. During a recess he asked to visit the court's law library, as he was running his own defence. Over the months, whilst he behaved as a model prisoner, "always very polite and personable", his guards had become slack. Though he was supposed to have four watching over him, often it was two, and sometimes just one. He had even been left alone in the courtroom. Bundy realised that, at certain points in the day, there were few people around and he could virtually walk out of the building.

A few days prior to his planned escape he had his hair cut, to look as different from his photos as possible. On the 7th he dressed with added clothes, including white shorts. His handcuffs were removed inside the courthouse, before he was taken to the courtroom. Though it was a stuffy day, nobody commented on his bulky sweater and appearance. At mid-morning recess, as the courtroom emptied, Bundy crossed to the law library at the back. The deputy watched him for a while, eventually going out for a cigarette in the hallway.

The first time Bundy approached the library window he saw a female reporter beneath. He walked around the room again, knowing that the next time he came to the open window it would be time to go. He climbed onto the ledge, positioned himself and jumped, escaping through a second-floor window that was routinely left open in warm weather.

He fled to safety down by the river, stripped to his shorts, pulled on a red bandana and bundled all his clothes into a makeshift pack that he threw over his shoulder. Then he walked casually through the small resort town and headed for the Aspern mountains. It took him an hour and, though there was a search in operation, he could not hear or see anything below, much to his amazement. Tracker dogs did set to work, but in the opposite direction – for they had picked up the scent of the female deputy who had brought Bundy a sweater, making straight for her home.

Bundy stayed free for six days, hiding out in a cabin for part of the time. But he had a poor sense of direction. He was looking for signs to Crested Butte, as he had plotted a course to the East Coast that used it as a starting point, but he continually missed his turns as he wandered around. Eventually, he stole a 1966 Cadillac and drove back into Aspern, down Main Street, and through to the pass. He wasn't to know that he could have driven straight out of town, as no roadblocks were there by that time. But he was nervous, and it was his erratic driving that attracted police attention. He was stopped and arrested by an officer who had regularly escorted Bundy back and forth from his cell to the court. They estimated he had covered fifty miles, going round and round, and lost thirty pounds in those six days.

They still did not know they had a serial killer on their hands. He was charming, witty, handsome and well-educated, and was studying law when he was first arrested. He certainly did not fit what most people assume to be the profile of a multiple murderer.

Bundy was again locked in the smaller Glenwood Springs jail. It seems he was able to acquire a hacksaw blade, probably from another inmate, as well as $500. In his cell, he sawed through the welds holding a metal plate in the ceiling over an old light fixture. It was a small hole, and the slim prisoner made huge efforts to shed even more weight until he was able to squeeze through into the crawlspace. Though the noise he made was noticed, it was never checked out.

In December, two days before Christmas, Bundy heard that his trial would start in early January in Colorado Springs. Time was running out for his escape bid. On 30 December, leaving books and files under his blanket to give the appearance he was asleep in his bed, Bundy dressed in thick, warm clothes and climbed into the crawlspace, before moving across to the jailer's apartment. It seems the jailer and his wife had gone out for the evening to see a film. Bundy climbed down into their linen cupboard and left via their front door.

To escape into the Colorado night in December was not a pleasant experience. It was cold, a snowstorm had started up. Bundy stole an old MG but it broke down. He had been looking for four hours for a car to steal, as he didn't know how to hotwire an ignition. In the end he hitched a lift into the town of Vail, and by chance saw a bus about to leave for Denver, where he took an early flight to Chicago. Seventeen hours after his escape, with Bundy neatly ensconced in Chicago, the guards in the little Glenwood Springs jail noticed that their sleeping charge was a pile of books, files and clothes. Discovery didn't occur until after noon, for Bundy had been declining breakfast, choosing to sleep late instead.

His final murderous spree was set to begin, leading to his ultimate arrest and eventual execution in Florida. During that short time-span, Bundy committed numerous petty crimes to finance his freedom, making his way across country until he stopped in Tallahassee, Florida, where he acquired documents to pose as a student, Kenneth Misner. In the early hours of 15 January 1978, he entered the state university's Chi Omega sorority house to bludgeon four sleeping young women, leaving two dead and the others seriously injured. One of the murdered girls had double bite-marks on her buttocks that matched Bundy's. All this was accomplished within thirty minutes. His next step was another house, not far away, where another female student was bludgeoned and left injured.

After lying low for a few weeks, Bundy moved on in early February to Lake City, where he abducted, raped and murdered a twelve-year-old girl. She was his last victim. He was stopped by a Pensacola policeman on 15 February, on suspicion of driving a stolen car.

It is similarly displeasing to hear how easily Belgian serial child rapist and murderer **Marc Dutroux** slipped away from his guards, in 1998 – even if, in the event, it was only for a few hours. The people of Belgium had been outraged that this infamous criminal, with his shameful slur on their national character, was allowed to travel twenty miles daily from his cell in Arlon to the courthouse in Neufchâteau to examine the prosecution files in preparation for his trial, protected by only three accompanying policemen – or, as was the case on the day he escaped in April 1998, just two. But it was his right to see the files, as there were so many that they could not make copies.

His escape was made whilst one of the officers was out of the room, collecting further files, and the other was dozing in a chair, enabling the unhindered Dutroux to grab the gun from his belt and flee the courthouse. Perhaps it was a small blessing that the gun was unloaded. Dutroux stole a car to escape. Whilst the alarm was raised immediately, resulting in five thousand police, helicopters and planes joining the search – including many from the neighbouring countries of France, Germany, Luxembourg and Holland – it was a forest warden who spotted the stolen car stuck in the mud. Tracker dogs caught up with Dutroux. After this incident, his files were brought to him in prison.

An earlier and altogether different European social threat, the Red Army Faction – or, as they were initially known in the media, the 'Baader-Meinhof gang' or 'group', to deny them military status – came into being in May 1970, when **Andreas Baader**, imprisoned in Tegel Prison, Berlin, for arson convictions, escaped from custody. At 8am on 14 May, Ulrike Meinhof, a well-known German journalist, had gone to the library at the Dahlem Institute for Social Research and asked to work there, as she had often done before. She was told that the main reading room was closed that day, because Baader was being brought from Tegel to conduct research on "the organisation of young people on the fringes of society". She said she knew of this, because she was collaborating on the research with him. No one checked that this was approved. Though Meinhof was sympathetic, she was not yet a member of Baader's militant leftwing group at this point.

Meinhof changed the furniture around, placing a chair for him next to hers, with their backs to the windows. At 9:30am Baader arrived in a car with his escort of two policemen. With some reluctance, they decided to release his handcuffs so that he could work. They checked the fastenings on the windows and sat either side of the main door. No one checked Meinhof's bag, which contained a gun.

A little later, there was a ring at the front door and two women, Irene Goergens and Ingrid Schubert, entered disguised in wigs. They were told they could work in the hallway until the reading room became vacant. They settled at a table. When the doorbell went again, they answered it and let in a masked man with a loaded Beretta, who shot one of the library personnel as he turned to run. The three of them burst into the library and scuffled with the police. In the commotion a teargas pistol was fired, whilst Baader and Meinhof jumped out of the window. The others followed, all making their way to a stolen silver Alfa Romeo, with fellow nascent terrorist Astrid Proll at the wheel.

Gerard Chapman was the criminal for whom the term 'Public Enemy Number One' was coined by a lawman in the 1920's, and then picked up by the newspapers way before the FBI began providing its 'Most Wanted' list. He escaped a number of times from custody, raising cheers in the picture-houses when newsreels reported his escapades. He was a conman but became a robber alongside his criminal mentor, Dutch Anderson, whom he met during one of his spells in prison.

Chapman lived the high life in Manhattan with fine clothes and expensive women. Educating himself with music and literature, he was known as 'the Count of Gramercy Park'. His first escape was probably the most spectacular, in that it had the touch of a showman. Caught for a robbery with his accomplice Anderson, after stealing five sacks of registered mail that totalled just over $1.4 million (the biggest haul in history at that time), they were taken to the main Post Office building for questioning. In the middle of the interrogation, Chapman yawned and stepped from his chair, dashed to the window with a "sorry gentlemen", went out onto the sill and was gone. Everyone rushed to the window and looked seventy-five feet down to the street, wondering how he could have survived the fall. Then a detective noticed a cleaner at the building opposite pointing frantically to the side of the window. Chapman had sidestepped and moved along the ledge to come back into the building via another window. He was recaptured four offices along.

It seems he had a talent for escaping through windows. When he was imprisoned another time, he feigned illness by drinking disinfectant in order to be moved to the prison hospital. There he escaped by going out of the window, using bed-sheets to lower himself. He was cornered two days later and shot a number of times in the process. His subsequent admission to the prison hospital was for valid reasons, a bullet having penetrated his kidney. It was feared he might die, but, six days later, he escaped in exactly the same way. He was now free to commit further crimes with his companion, for Anderson had tunnelled out of Atlanta State Penitentiary around the same time.

However, he was later captured with another man whom he unwisely chose as his new accomplice. When the accomplice was caught after they killed a policeman during a failed robbery, he boldly boasted that Chapman was his partner. That was to be Chapman's final crime. Such was the adulation for the man that bouquets arrived daily, right up until his execution in 1926.

Prison Break

The escape of **Brian Nichols** from Fulton County courthouse in Atlanta owed little to cunning and finesse, and more to sheer violence and brutality. On 11 March 2005, Cynthia Hall, aged fifty-one, a five-foot two sheriff's deputy, had just removed Nichols' handcuffs, to enable him to change from prison uniform into civilian clothes for a court appearance, when he attacked her and grabbed her gun. He used enough violence to put her in hospital with head injuries, placing her in a critical condition. It seems surprising that she was the only guard for a six-foot one black male, weighing two hundred and ten pounds, who was facing life imprisonment on a retrial for charges of rape, false imprisonment, sodomy, possession of a machinegun and handgun, and large quantities of marijuana. Added to that, he had been caught in court, two days earlier, with two handmade knives in his shoes.

Having overpowered the guard, his escape attempt took the lives of the judge, a court reporter, a police officer and a US Customs agent. Nichols started his bid for freedom by making his way across to the old courthouse via a skybridge and entering the private chambers of Judge Rowland Barnes, where he overpowered another officer, removed his weapon and entered the courtroom behind the judge's bench, shooting Barnes in the head, doing likewise to the court reporter as he made his exit. Nichols managed to go down eight floors of a stairwell whilst being chased by another deputy, whom he shot and killed once they were outside.

A number of cars were hijacked, the first being a towtruck obtained at gunpoint outside the courtroom. Another was a Honda Accord that he took from a reporter, whom he pistol-whipped to obtain the vehicle. He abandoned that car before he had even left the parking area, switching to another.

Twenty-seven miles north of Atlanta, in Duluth, Georgia, Nichols approached Ashley Smith at an apartment complex and forced her into her bathroom where he tied her up, placing a towel over her head whilst he took a shower. Fearing for her life, she struck up a rapport with the man over several hours, telling him about her five-year-old daughter. Though he wanted marijuana, she only had methamphetamine to offer, as she was addicted but was trying to get clean. She read to him from the Bible and from a book that inspired her, Rick Warren's *The Purpose Driven Life*. She told him how her husband had died in her arms after a brawl a few years before, and showed him a large scar across her torso from a drug-fuelled car crash.

She was undoubtedly having some effect on Nichols, and was trying to convince him to surrender. She made him pancakes for breakfast, and he let her leave to visit her daughter, who had been taken from her as a result of her drug use. Smith then phoned the police, and the apartment was soon surrounded by all manner of agents. Nichols surrendered peacefully.

Today, at this point in writing, the new trial has still not begun, for fifty-four charges and eleven scenes-of-crime are now involved (including the courtroom, which has been sealed off ever since the murders), and the defence has become so complex and costly to the taxpayer that there are fears the trial may never really take place.

Wayne Carlson became an escapee after his first conviction for stealing cars in 1960, when he was eighteen years old. His total number of escapes to date is thirteen, both in the United States and Canada.

His life has been a series of petty robberies and imprisonments, with most escape methods employed: sawing through bars, climbing down a sheet rope and over the fence (Regina Correctional Centre, 1970); locking up seven sheriffs and five prisoners, armed with a .38 Smith & Wesson (Burlington Correctional Centre, 1973); sawing through bars and tying up a guard (Windsor State Prison, 1974); making a key to doors (Fort Saskatchewan, 1976); leaving a dummy in bed, hiding under piles of dirt in the yard and cutting through a fence (Stony Mountain Penitentiary, Manitoba, 1982); failing to return on a day pass (Bowden Institution, Alberta, 1987).

In 1974, Carlson was reminded of Dillinger's wooden gun escape when he saw an inmate carving a pipe with the end of an Exacto blade. He wanted a gun that looked real head-on, not just from the side. "He'd placed silver paper from a cigarette package into each chamber of the cylinder," Carlson later wrote, "so when I looked into the front end of the revolver, it appeared to be loaded. [He] had burned the wood and then blackened it further with shoe polish, giving it a dull, gunmetal shine."

Carlson wanted to use the fake weapon to break out of an upcoming court appearance. He pondered how to get a gun, fake or otherwise, past the various security searches when he changed from his prison clothes to his own for court. He reckoned he could get through the superficial body pat if the search was cursory enough by placing the gun in his pants and winding elastic bandage around his body.

To avoid the closer skin search he created a scene, refusing to go to court when they came for him, getting into a temper and offering a display of aggression by smashing a table so that they grabbed him, performed only a perfunctory body pat and fixed him in a belly chain, his hands linked to his waist. When they placed him in a room to change his clothes he created another scene, until in the end they were pleased to let him be taken to the van in his prison denims with no skin search made.

Having made the guards nervous by suggesting he was going to court in connection with a cop-killing charge in Canada, he was taken into the courtroom with his handcuffs removed but his chains left on. He was actually there to receive sentence for his recent escapes. After receiving three-to-seven years, he relaxed with his guards and said he needed to go to the toilet 'bad'. In the toilet, the guard thought their man was tame enough to let him step into the middle cubicle.

Carlson removed his fake gun and leapt out, thrusting the weapon in the guard's face, dropping it to his stomach before he could realise it was a fake. He tried to reach for the officer's gun, but the guard twisted away. He then tried to outmanoeuvre the guard, saying he just wanted him to put his gun down on the floor. Once it was down, Carlson snatched it up and checked to see if it was loaded. "As I looked into the cylinder I glimpsed semi-wad-cutter ammunition. Semi-wad-cutter bullets are indented instead of pointed, and the slugs immediately expand on impact with flesh and bone, leaving huge gaping wounds in their wake. As soon as I saw the slugs I put my gun in my pocket and used his. I pulled the hammer back and left it on full cock."

Carlson then took the officer and his companion, who was waiting outside in the corridor, from the courthouse. Going out the back way, they walked unhindered across the lawn and into the underground parking lot. Once the other guard was disarmed, they climbed into the car, with Carlson taking the wheel. Though the guards were in the back, he warned them of the damage their guns loaded with semi-wad cutters would do if he had to use them. Carlson drove out the city and up the Interstate, his foot down hard, knowing they wouldn't try to jump him at that speed. Later he turned them out of the vehicle. His recapture brought much media attention.

In 1999, he was finally let out on parole and was apparently developing a new life, having written a book and been involved in a prison suicide prevention programme and other activist work, as well as getting married – not once, but twice. But the dice didn't seem to roll right. Carlson slipped into drinking and smoking marijuana, broke his parole stipulations via possession of a gun, and was sent back inside in 2004. He will be seventy-three when he emerges from jail, unless he finds another way out.

Larry Marley, the IRA activist, registers on the roll-call of escapees for his breakout from a courthouse, where he was already being charged with attempting to escape from prison. He had been arrested dressed as a British army patrolman after making his way, with some comrades, through the compound at Long Kesh, where they moved unimpeded until they reached the last gate. They were taken to the Newry courthouse on 11 March 1975. There, in the holding cell, they discovered that the bars on the toilet window were rusted. The ten prisoners broke them and went out into the yard, though not before scrawling, "Up the IRA" in soap on the mirror. An electricity transformer provided the climbing frame to get over the fencing, most of them making the long drop over the barricade uninjured, after which they stole cars and headed for the Irish border.

If we direct our attention to the American Wild West, we come across tales of escapes from the jailhouse at every turn. **Henry McCarty, a.k.a. William H. Bonney**, was as famous for his escapes as for his short career as an outlaw and gunman, better known as 'Billy the Kid'. Bonney (the name he regularly used) also continually escaped his pursuers, but it is his custodial escapes that concern us. As so much is written about him, there is also confusion as to what is fact, fiction or myth.

His first escape was at fifteen, when he was locked up in Silver City for a robbery. The sheriff probably thought he was too young to be kept in a cell, and allowed him the run of the corridor outside. When the sheriff's back was turned, Bonney was up the chimney. He seems to have escaped whatever jail he was put in. The most famous escape attributed to him occurred in April 1881, and was to be his last. He was taken to the Lincoln County Courthouse, guarded by two men,

James W. Bell and Robert Ollinger, and kept in handcuffs and leg irons in a room on the second floor.

There seem to be variations in the story, but one account is that he was returning from the toilet out back in the yard, accompanied by Bell. Despite his chains he got ahead of the guard, slipped his handcuffs and turned to hit Bell with them, reaching for his gun first and shooting him dead. Ollinger, who had taunted Bonney and hoped to kill him with his new shotgun, heard the shot across the street at a restaurant. Bonney had already taken Ollinger's shotgun from the office and drew his attention from a window, before blasting the returning deputy. He removed his shackles and rode away at a leisurely trot, on a borrowed horse – it was returned two days later. As they say, the rest is history. Outlaw-turned-lawman Pat Garrett was called and set off in pursuit, later gunning Bonney down in a darkened room.

The life of **Christopher Evans** (who, in partnership with the Sontag brothers, was the leader of a gang known as the California Outlaws) is a great story in itself, but for our purposes here, this legendary train robber and great nemesis of Southern Pacific Railroads (robbing the company's safes on board, but never the passengers – or even the US Mail) was almost lured into an escape from jail so that he could be gunned down by railroad detectives and their henchmen, to save their greedy company any further trouble.

The man who had been instructed to arrange the escape was Ed Morrell, who worked as a spy for the gang because he was acquainted with the detectives. He decided to frustrate the railroad's plan by bringing the escape bid forward by twenty-four hours. Morrell, who worked in the restaurant across the road from the Fresno County Jail, turned up with Evans' evening meal on 28 December 1893. Evans was awaiting transfer to Folsom Prison to serve a life sentence.

Beneath the platter was a gun. Morrell joined Evans as they guided the jailer down Mariposa Street to reach a team and buggy tied up a block away. Evans needed to be helped because, prior to being returned to custody, he had been involved that same year in a mighty gun battle at the Stone Corral in which George Sontag had been killed whilst Evans, despite being riddled with bullets, had survived – though he needed his arm to be amputated, an eye removed, and he was left with some brain damage from the shotgun pellets that entered his head.

Evans' flight was closer to a hobble. It was freezing winter, but at least he was helped by many sympathetic residents of the area, until the reward was raised high enough to bring forth a betrayer. Evans was returned to prison where he stayed until 1911, before being released to live out his final years with his family.

When the police station is used to hold prisoners today, one may not think that a gun could be passed directly to set a breakout into operation. **Bonnie Parker** may have been able to hand a gun through the bars to **Clyde Barrow** as late as 1930, but things today are surely more complex with regard to security. Nevertheless, guns are still smuggled in along with the full array of tools needed for escape.

Nikolaus Chrastny offers us a good view of how the system can be a lot less smart than the criminal whose sole intent is to escape. Scotland Yard and Customs officers had a problem when they arrested Chrastny in 1987. He named his drug smuggling partner as Roy Garner, a villain and alleged police informer, and further alleged that Garner had a useful friend in Detective Superintendent Tony Lundy (subsequently allowed to retire on health grounds with full pension and good service medal). At stake was the smashing of a major cocaine smuggling ring. To protect their star informer, with whom they were doing a deal, Customs officers moved him out of

London. They handed him over to the police in South Yorkshire, who would hide him in a police station in Rotherham where they could interview him quietly over a period of time, and where it was less likely that others would try to either rescue or silence him.

Chrastny was kept in a normal cell, but fraternised with the police officers so easily that they feared they might become complacent and their prisoner's situation be jeopardised. He was moved to Dewsbury police station and the safety of the West Yorkshire police (who had earlier looked after the Yorkshire Ripper), housed in a section usually reserved for female prisoners. Though Chrastny was under arrest and regarded as a dangerous, high-security risk, he was also treated as a guest because of his status as high-level informant or 'supergrass'. He received privileges such as a television set and a stereo hi-fi. The only problem was that the cells were not equipped with electric plugs, and for these appliances to be of any use required a lead to run from his cell to a plug in the room opposite, the doctor's office. This meant that his cell door had to be left open, along with that of the doctor's room. The only barrier to freedom was the gate that closed between his cell door and the hallway.

Chrastny's wife, Charlotte, visited him regularly, even sharing a meal with him in the jail. She was such a regular presence that they stopped searching her, and she would bring in beer, cigars, extra food and books. It is believed that two hacksaw files were concealed by her in the spine of the Sherlock Holmes novel, *The Hound of the Baskervilles*. To fill in the hours between interviews with the Customs officers, Chrastny requested model-making equipment, including Plasticine, paint, glue and Blu-Tak. He put them to good use, though not in making models. With background music to drown out his activities, at night he sawed through the bars of the outer gate of his cell and filled the gaps temporarily with Plasticine. Fortunately, he was just finishing his preparations when he was informed, in early October, that within a few days he would be moved back to London to appear in court. That night he carefully removed the bars and went through the gate, replacing them so as not to make it too easy to trace his path. Then he crossed the hallway into the medical room, which was unlocked because of his electrical lead. As the window had no bars, he moved rapidly out and into the police station yard, climbing the gate. It is believed he was met by a car.

At 11:30am the next morning, when the prisoner had his breakfast brought to him in bed, along with his morning newspaper, he seemed to be fast asleep. When the police returned twenty minutes later, an accompanying inspector accidentally kicked the gate, dislodging one of the bars. In the empty bed was a note: "Gentlemen, I have not taken this step lightly. I have been planning it for several weeks. The tools have been in my wash-kit for several years in preparation for such an occasion." Later that day he phoned Dewsbury police station and repeated his apologies.

That is the last anyone has heard of Chrastny on these shores. Everyone involved blamed someone else's unprofessional behaviour. And everyone cursed how the opportunity to haul in an international drug ring had been botched. So who had helped him? His associates? Corrupt Scotland Yard detectives, who may have had a lot to lose by his evidence? Or his wife Charlotte, a former German policewoman, who visited him not long before he escaped? She was later to receive a seven-year jail sentence, not for aiding and abetting her husband's escape, of which she was acquitted – but for conspiracy to import and distribute cocaine.

Arthur Hutchinson had planned to escape from court in September 1983. He even told his two-man escort, when they took him from Armley Prison in Leeds to Selby Magistrates' Court for his fifth appearance, that he would be escaping that day. They laughed.

But when they arrived, the desk sergeant, the only person on duty, was busy with two juvenile absconders and buzzed in the prisoner with the warder handcuffed to him. Hutchinson was taken to the interview room. Whilst they were busy counting out £120 that he had brought with him, Hutchinson asked for the toilet. They unlocked his cuffs and he went to use the toilet in the next cell. Or so they thought.

Actually, he had gone up the stairs to the courts. As soon as they realised, the police ran round the front, expecting him to appear through the public entrance. But Hutchinson knew the layout of the place from his previous visits. He was also fortunate in that some doors were unlocked, as the court was undergoing redecorating work. He went straight into the courtroom, startling the decorator, ran across the press bench and dived headlong through the window. It was closed. Glass went everywhere as he fell six feet onto the wire netting over the police station exercise yard. Then he dropped onto the roof of a van, crossed the schoolyard next door and escaped into the streets of Selby. No major search was put in operation. He had convictions for petty theft and sex with underage girls, and his current charges were rape and burglary, but he was probably not regarded as dangerous.

What followed would change all that. Unsurprisingly, when he dived through the glass window and landed on the wire below he made a four-inch gash in his leg. It became infected, so he went to the Royal Infirmary in Doncaster to have it treated. They told him to return in two days, when he was given antibiotics. He continued moving around the area, eventually sharing a room at a guesthouse in Sheffield with two others. It had been four weeks, and the police had focused no press or media attention on him at all.

It seems that he met an eighteen-year-old, Nicola Laitner, in a pub in Sheffield, and she told him of her sister's wedding at their home in Dore. Perhaps she invited him, casually or purposely. In any case, Hutchinson arrived late at the house on 24 October 1983, when the family were recovering after the day's wedding celebrations. A marquee still stood in the garden. It seems that Hutchinson wasted no time in killing wealthy solicitor Basil Laitner, his wife, Avril, and their elder son, Richard, using a Bowie knife, and then turned his attention to the daughter, Nicola, raping her twice, in her bed and in the marquee. He then robbed the house of cash and jewellery, before departing.

On the run, Hutchinson phoned his mother. The call was monitored and, once the police realised that he was injured, they played up the wound to the media, indicating that it was serious, that gangrene would develop and amputation would result. In fact it was not a major injury, if looked after properly. In any case, Hutchinson was captured in a field near his hometown in the Northeast, trapped by police dogs.

IV
Not Stopping

The possibility of escaping from custody would seem to be even more pronounced with home leave, when prisoners are allowed to go back to the nest for whatever reason. This has undoubtedly occurred down the years, though not always as directly as in the case of **Percy Lefroy**, a.k.a. Percy Mapleton. He has the distinction of being Britain's second railway murderer, after Franz Müller. Lefroy robbed and killed an elderly man, Isaac Gold, in June 1881 on the London to Brighton line. He wasn't initially arrested, spinning the story that he was also attacked on the train, as the body of Gold was not discovered until later in a tunnel. Lefroy was escorted back to London by a detective, who was told not to let him out of his sight while they continued their investigations. But Lefroy was sharp enough to convince his escort not only to make a detour to his lodgings, near Croydon, but to wait outside on the front doorstep whilst he went in to change his clothes. The detective's wait was a long one, as Lefroy escaped immediately through the back door.

Unfortunately for Lefroy, *The Daily Telegraph* made history by publishing the first portrait of a wanted man. It led to many false arrests. In the end, Lefroy's downfall was by his own hand, traced from a telegram sent to his employer asking for his outstanding wages. (Other accounts say that he was found in a house in Stepney where the blinds were permanently drawn, its occupant only going out at night.)

Noel 'Razor' Smith, a career criminal, claims that if he had been shown a little basic human trust then he would not have taken a holiday from prison. He recounts in his autobiography, *A Few Kind Words and a Loaded Gun*, how he managed to slip away on a home visit in November 1992. His mother was ill, having been in hospital a couple of times. He was allowed to visit, but, rather than being given a one-day parole, which he says he would have honoured, he was taken by taxi with an escort of two prison officers, who were handcuffed to him with instructions that under no conditions were they to let him go free.

They drove from the Verne prison in Dorset to south London's Stockwell Park Estate, a destination, he notes, that didn't thrill either the taxi driver or his escort, all of whom wanted to get away as soon as possible. Having negotiated their way past the local youths on the stairwell, the warders were relieved to knock at the door of the family flat. Smith's father looked straight at the handcuffs and stated that if they intended bringing in his son the cuffs had to go, or else they could turn around and go straight back – which would have been difficult, as the taxi had driven off to safer pastures for a couple of hours.

The cuffs were released and the officers directed into the kitchen, provided with daily newspapers and drinks, whilst Smith went into the living room to see his mother and other members of the family who were gathered there. He informed them he was not returning to prison that night, and was shown how to get out of the window and down to the balcony below. He knew it wouldn't be long before his escape was known. Brixton police had been notified of his day trip and would have had contingency plans ready for any escape bid. "I wasn't just some burglar or car thief coming onto their patch, I was a long-term prisoner with a proven propensity for loaded firearms."

Not surprisingly, no sooner had Smith made for a local pub and downed a drink than he could see police activity outside the windows. He managed to escape by calling a cab and ducking into the back seat, his sympathetic driver (whose brother was in the local prison) taking him, albeit temporarily, to a safer area.

V
Who Goes There?

Impersonation as a way to escape prison is another tried and tested method. But impersonating a dead man belongs to an earlier era, as it would be more complicated to pull it off today. But that is what the highwayman **John Nevison** achieved in the mid-seventeenth century. Our idea of the highwayman is generally of a good-natured rogue. We think of Dick Turpin dressed in finery and crying, "Stand and deliver!" Today we may even sometimes associate the idea of the highwayman with armed robbers, hoping to bestow a more light-hearted image. Yet of course Turpin was rough and violent, far from being a chivalrous man who charmed all the women he encountered on his hold-ups. By all accounts, it seems that Nevison, another highwayman from the period, would have been a better candidate for our imaginings.

Nevison went to the gallows for murder, but was generally no more than a spirited and renowned robber, with many amusing tales of his exploits abounding. Most relevant to us here is his escape from Leicester gaol, where he was being held for his thievery. Before

Nevison was even brought to trial he pretended to be ill, giving the impression he had been struck by the plague. A physician friend who came to visit confirmed that this was indeed the case, and suggested Nevison be removed immediately for fear that he would infect everyone and bring death upon the whole place, prisoners and staff alike.

Nevison was separated from the others, given his own cell and attended by a nurse and his friend the physician, who visited a couple of times each day. As his condition appeared to deteriorate so the sense of despair grew, to the extent that the wife of the jailer forbade her husband or any of their servants to go any closer than the door of the cell.

The next step in the plot was for some of Nevison's other friends to visit, one of whom was a painter, who brought with him the tools of his art. Treating the prisoner as his canvas, he added various marks and blue spots to indicate that death from the plague was approaching. Finally, the stage was set and the physician administered a preparation that gave Nevison the appearance of death – at least for an hour or two. Time enough for a coffin to be brought and the contagious corpse to be removed. Witnesses brought in to confirm his death were afraid for their own lives and refrained from stepping too close.

There was a downside to being dead, as Nevison was to discover. When he resumed his career staging hold-ups, those he encountered who had heard of his demise now believed they were being confronted by a ghost. Once the whole saga was uncovered, the jailer was instructed to go out and catch Nevison. (The myth surrounding Nevison lingers today, particularly in Yorkshire, where sightings of his ghost are still reported.)

One wonders whether **Frank Abagnale** could have succeeded in faking his own death, for his ingenuity compels one to suspend disbelief, as if we really have encountered a modern day version of those mythical characters of the past. Abagnale's escape through impersonation was partly due to luck and partly to being smart enough to take advantage of circumstances.

After he was captured in Canada, as detailed earlier, he was handed over at the US-Canadian border and taken to the Federal Detention Centre in Atlanta to await trial. This was in spring 1971. At the time there was a lot of activity and concern about conditions in prisons from civil rights groups, congressional committees and Justice Department agents. Clandestine investigations were in operation, and there was a fear that prison inspectors were being planted in the jails. Abagnale responded accordingly. By chance, when he arrived at the Atlanta prison, the US Marshal escorting him did not have the right papers. He had to more or less force his prisoner into the place, telling them to house and feed him until he came back. Suspicious from the start, they gave Abagnale better treatment and food than the others, fearing the worst. He understood their fears when he read in the local newspapers that two of their officers had recently lost their jobs.

Abagnale asked a friend to visit and pose as his fiancée. She brought with her the business card of Inspector Dunlap of the US Bureau of Prisons in Washington, obtained by posing as a freelance writer investigating fire safety measures in federal detention centres. With permission she passed it over the barrier to Abagnale. On another visit she handed over the card of the FBI agent in charge of Abagnale's case, the contact number of which she had altered. Later, Abagnale congratulated his guards on their cleverness and admitted that he was indeed an inspector, handing them Dunlap's card.

It was 9pm, and the office telephone number would not be picked up if they tried to verify his credentials. Abagnale asked to see the lieutenant in charge that night, and he was taken to his office, where he allayed suspicions about his role and confirmed that his report would exonerate the prison. Having caught them off-guard, he stated that he needed to talk urgently to an FBI agent and asked them to reach him on the phone. He handed over the agent's card and said he would still be at his desk. The lieutenant phoned. Abignale's friend answered and carried off the FBI role. The number was actually a payphone in an Atlanta shopping mall.

Abagnale claimed he needed to see the FBI agent immediately as he had obtained information that could not be given over the phone. Covering the mouthpiece, he asked if it would be possible to step outside the prison, as the FBI didn't want to enter and compromise the undercover operation. The lieutenant agreed. When a red and white Buick arrived outside the prison, Abagnale was led down the back way, using the staff elevator, and allowed to walk out to his female friend disguised as a man behind the wheel.

She drove Abagnale straight to a greyhound bus bound for New York. "Frank Abagnale, known to police the world over as the Skywayman and who once flushed himself down an airline toilet to elude officers, is at large again," ran one prominent press story. Still determined to reach Brazil, he had to bide his time before trying to obtain a flight. Unfortunately for Abagnale, in his movements across the country he checked into a motel where the receptionist was a former airline stewardess who recognised him from an earlier con, when he pretended to be a member of the aircrew. She called the police, but he slipped through the net by stating he was an FBI agent looking for one of his colleagues. Abagnale was remarkable, in that he excelled in such con artistry since the age of sixteen.

Just like Abagnale, **Charles Victor Thompson**'s personable character seems to have enabled him to carry off an audacious escape from prison through impersonation. In November 2005, Thompson was being temporarily housed at the Harris County Jail in Houston, Texas, following a re-sentencing hearing in connection with the killing of his former girlfriend and her new partner. He had managed to retain the street clothes he had worn in court, and it seems he had these with him when he went for a meeting with his attorney. Except that the attorney did not show – assuming Thompson had ever arranged to meet him in the first place.

The unit where the meeting was to take place had the highest security in the jail, as it was also the section that had the greatest potential for escape bids. Once in the booth, Thompson slipped out of his handcuffs, changed from his orange jumpsuit into his street clothes and then left the booth, brazenly walking towards the exit, passing four checks in the process by showing a fake ID badge purporting to be from the Texas Attorney General's office. Then he vanished. He was caught a few days later in Louisiana, the worse for drink. He had obtained food, clothing and money by claiming to be an evacuee from Hurricane Katrina.

Walking out of prison only works if one can carry the conviction of one's fake identity. Perhaps the most remarkable example of impersonation is of the inmate in Northern Ireland who made a costume from cabbage leaves, with the intent to crawl out disguised as a row of cabbages. It doesn't seem to have worked.

Danny Ray 'Rambo' Horning seems to have found it relatively easy to walk out of Arizona State Prison in Florence, near Phoenix, wearing the smock of a medical technician in May 1992. Horning, who was serving four life sentences for bank robbery, kidnapping and aggravated assault, then headed for the remote parts of northern Arizona, acquiring food and equipment from cabins along the way. His survival tactics, learned whilst serving in the army, also included eluding and confusing dogs by backtracking in circles and figures of eight through the backcountry of the Coconino National Forest and Grand Canyon National Park.

Horning also made fools of his pursuers by leaving notes ridiculing them and daring police to catch him, just like a villain from the *Batman* comics. Fifty-four days later he was captured near Sedona, after what he described as an enjoyable experience that he wished could have gone on longer – a view that may not have been shared by some of the tourists in the National Park he felt compelled to kidnap during his flight, even if no one was injured.

Though one reads periodically of inmates who dress as women and slip out at visiting times, if you are one of twins then you have another option to pull a fast one – even if you are as conspicuously infamous as the Kray brothers. **Ronnie Kray** escaped after being committed to Long Grove Hospital, near Epsom, Surrey, in 1958. He had been admitted in February, having had a schizophrenic breakdown. He received treatment and, by May, felt he should be returned to Winchester Prison to complete his sentence. The doctors refused his request.

The brothers then decided to play a trick that had worked at other times. One Sunday afternoon, when visitors flocked to the hospital to visit their relatives, Ronnie received two cars of visitors. A patient was only allowed two visitors at a time, however. In the first car, an electric blue Lincoln, were his twin Reggie and an old family friend, Georgie Osborne. In the second, a black Ford, were several unnamed friends: "one was a safe blower, two were ex-boxers, and the man at the wheel was known for his skill as a smash-and-grab-raid driver," notes the Krays' biographer, John Pearson, in *The Profession of Violence*. They parked both cars outside Ronnie's block. Explaining to the porter that they hadn't realised only two visitors were allowed, those in the Ford said they would wait until Reggie and Osborne had visited. Reggie entered wearing a light-fawn raincoat and went to visit Ronnie. Ronnie was dressed smartly in a blue suit and maroon tie. His brother had brought holiday snaps for them to enjoy and Ronnie was having a good laugh, the male nurse on duty noted.

Prison Break

At 3:30pm tea was brewed in the scullery along the corridor. Patients were not allowed to go beyond the ward doors during visiting times, so visitors had to collect their tea and biscuits. That Sunday, the Kray twin wearing the fawn coat went out, acknowledged by the nurse. After twenty minutes no one had returned with the tea, and the nurse realised something was wrong. He went up to the one he thought was his patient and asked after his brother, Reggie. The twin replied that he *was* Reggie, and he could prove it with his driving licence. Then the nurse realised Ronnie had gone out for tea and had kept right on going, out of the block ... into the black Ford, and away to London. Nothing could be done. Ronnie and Reggie had arranged earlier to wear the same suit and tie, and had switched the coat when the nurse wasn't looking.

Though the police came and questioned Reggie and his friend, they could do nothing. "It's not as if we actually done anything. We've just been sitting here waiting for a cup of tea that never came."

The rules on prisoners certified as insane at the time stated that anyone who escaped and remained at liberty for more than six weeks had to be recertified, once recaptured. The idea was for Ronnie to lay low for a couple of months, cause no problems, then give himself up and go back to prison to finish his sentence, his certification having lapsed. Though those six weeks became fraught, ultimately Ronnie gave himself up, and, though his certificate had lapsed, still received treatment for his problems. Eventually he went back to Wandsworth, to complete his sentence prior to release.

Steven Ray Russell has escaped from prison countless times, his main method being to impersonate others. He is another inmate who has had the tag 'Houdini' attached to him. As we will see, he seems to be equally adept as a con artist. One time he impersonated a judge and had his own bond reduced from $900,000 to $45,000, which he then paid directly, and vanished.

One report suggests that he always makes his escapes on a Friday the 13th, which suggests that there are only one or two days in a year when he requires extra vigilance if in prison or custody at the time. Like Willie Sutton, whom we will meet later, he uses the 'obvious' approach, dressing as a civilian and just walking out of the prison. This is what he did in Harris County Jail in Houston, May 1993, having studied when guard activity was at its lowest, least attentive and most incompetent. Clutching a walkie-talkie to partly hide his face, but also to give him an authoritative appearance, he walked out along with the visitors.

Another time, in 1996, whilst attending art classes, he removed green Magic Marker pens so that he could dye his white uniform green, the same colour as the medical staff. He left as a doctor. And again, when he was under arrest, he feigned a heart attack and managed to phone on a mobile from his bed to impersonate an FBI agent, instructing the agent guarding him outside the hospital room that the prisoner in the bed (Russell) was no longer under suspicion and that he, the agent, could leave the hospital and go home.

The most contrived of his escapes started in the prison library where Russell read up on AIDS, realising that, if he took laxatives, he could generate some of the symptoms. He also forged a medical document to confirm his diagnosis, and convinced the prison doctors he had a special needs parole to a hospital in Houston. His date for departure to the hospital was Friday 13 March. In his efforts to cover his traces once and for all, Russell acted as the doctor who had placed him under his special care and informed the authorities of his own death. Unfortunately, a fake lawyer ID card was discovered bearing Russell's photo and the file was not closed.

Many of his escapes are unverified as yet in their detail, unsurprisingly for someone who lives by deception. But Russell has something of Frank Abagnale about him. Rather than take menial jobs between his periods in prison, he has been bold enough to fabricate elaborate ploys to obtain high-level employment with sizeable wages. One executive of a medical management company said, "Russell was the best chief financial officer we ever had" – neglecting to add that he also stole large sums from the company.

VI
Up and Over

Whitemoor Prison in Cambridgeshire attracted attention after three escapees sued for damages with regard to the injuries they sustained as they were being apprehended. In September 1994, six men armed with two guns smuggled into the high-security prison made a break, going through a perimeter wire fence and climbing the wall with a seventeen-foot ladder made from knotted sheets. Apparently the fence had already been cut, suggesting that someone working at the prison had done it as no one else had access. (Video footage from the CCTV cameras was found to be missing.) The escapees were five IRA men – **Gilbert McNamee**, **Liam McCotter**, **Paul Magee**, **Liam O'Duibhir** and **Peter Sherry** – and an armed robber, **Andrew Russell**. Four were caught in the adjoining railyard, the other two within a few hours by the police in the fenlands nearby.

McNamee, McCotter and Russell took the Home Office to court, stating that, once apprehended and handcuffed, they were beaten with batons and repeatedly punched and kicked. Russell stated that whilst one officer sat on his back and arms, lifting his head back, another kicked him in the face. The officers claimed that injuries were sustained in the rough and tumble of escape, shinning the rope or falling from the wall. None of the escapees had resisted arrest.

Whilst such claims are regularly made by escapees after capture, let alone at other times within their custodial period, this time the penal establishment was shocked to find that the prisoners were believed and the officers were not. Evidence that should have been available to refute their claims had gone missing – in particular, the recording of the perimeter fence during the contentious period, as well as videotapes which could have shown how their injuries occurred, plus information from the Category A prisoners' log books. The prisoners were awarded damages in the High Court in January 2001.

On 3 January 1995, an escape from Parkhurst Prison on the Isle of Wight had the effect of increasing security in British prisons. On that day, three high-security prisoners escaped with ease. **Matthew Williams, Keith Rose** and **Andrew Rodger** had slipped away from a keep-fit class in the prison gymnasium. Using a replica key, they opened a back door and walked a hundred and fifty yards to the workshop where they had earlier prepared a ladder. After assembling it, they took cutters and made for the perimeter fence, going through it and climbing over the wall with their twenty-five-foot ladder. It was two hours before they were missed, time enough to have left the island by ferry or boat. However, they were discovered five days later living rough in a garden shed nearby. Their intention had been to steal a small Cessna plane from a local airfield, as Rose was an amateur pilot.

Later that year, in June, Keith Rose was able to phone in live from his new jail in Full Sutton, near York, to tell BBC Radio 4's *The World at One* programme a thing or two – such as how they copied the key from the prison's governor, who had a habit of waving keys under their noses wherever he lectured them. He also acknowledged how easy it was to build a ladder, and indeed how easy the whole operation had been. Rose said that they took their inspiration from the escape at Whitemoor a few months before. He also noted how surprised they were not to be missed within fifteen minutes. Their only problem, he recalled, was outside the prison, when they failed to steal a plane. By phoning out to a live BBC radio programme, he also demonstrated how easy it was to do something that a Category A prisoner should not have been able to accomplish.

As has already been stated, the Great Train Robbery owes its stature not only to the crime itself, but also to its afterlife, particularly the escapes by Charlie Wilson and **Ronnie Biggs**. Biggs, as most know, was a small fish in the actual robbery, but his escape from prison, and his very public world-media profile, has moved him gradually towards the endgame of returning freely, in ill health, to his motherland – to be incarcerated in Belmarsh Prison, as some form of last-ditch stand by the forces of law and order to underline that crime doesn't pay.

Though Wilson had already accomplished an audacious escape in August 1964, Biggs was to add to the tally in an equally unusual way. He had the good fortune to meet Paul Seabourne, an experienced escapee, inside Wandsworth Prison. Seabourne was about to finish his sentence and agreed to engineer the escape from outside. The idea was to plant a furniture removal van outside the prison, with a hinged platform that could be raised from its roof and brought up the necessary five feet to the height of the wall, from which rope ladders could be dropped when the inmates were on exercise in the yard. Biggs instructed his wife to provide the finance, £10,000 from his 'Train' earnings.

Biggs' accomplice was **Eric Flower**, whom he had met earlier in Wormwood Scrubs, and with whom he had tried to escape at that time, though both were caught chipping a bar out of a window. As Flower was awaiting his appeal, he received daily visits and could pass messages back and forth.

Within a few weeks of his release, Paul Seabourne had everything ready, and on 8 July 1965 the escape was set in motion.

That afternoon, Biggs and Flower were lingering in the prison yard with the escape-risk prisoners, wearing their yellow fluorescent patches, when, at 3:10pm, Seabourne and an accomplice, Ronnie Black, appeared at the top of the wall with ladders and shotgun cover. Not only did Biggs and Flower see their arrival, so did some officers. However, they were prevented from reaching the wall by two other inmates, Johnny Sullivan and Brian Stone, who had been paid by Biggs to impede the guards. Biggs and Flower went up the ladders and over the wall, dropping through the van roof onto a pile of mattresses. Then they shot out of the van and into a waiting car, driven by Ronnie Leslie.

As with the best-laid plans, things did not go quite right. Two other inmates, **Robert Anderson** and **Patrick Doyle,** took the opportunity presented by the ladders. Seabourne had intended to torch the van and, though he had started to soak the mattresses with petrol, the addition of the two newcomers delayed matters and the vital toss of the match never happened. Both Seabourne and Leslie left their prints and were later caught.

The escape had been planned for the day before, but was called off at the last minute when it started to rain suddenly and the prisoners were not allowed out to exercise. Seabourne had already come to the area and, not wishing to waste his trip, made a tour of local phone-boxes, disabling them to prevent the possibility of unhelpful emergency calls to the police the next day. Only after the fact did they discover that the prison had no direct link to the local police, and guards had to dial 999 like anyone else. It was twenty minutes before any police arrived on the escape scene.

By that time Biggs and Flower had reached safety in Dulwich, having switched from their Zephyr to a Cortina, and then given Anderson and Doyle the use of the Cortina to continue on their way. It broke down and they split up. Anderson went to Atlantic Machines, off Tottenham Court Road, where one of his friends, former escapee Patsy Fleming, had told him to make contact if he ever needed help. Anderson turned up at Atlantic spread-eagled across the bonnet of their van. He was taken in, given a change of clothes and some money. (Stanley Baker, the celebrated film actor, was there at the time and contributed appropriately.) 'Mad' Frankie Fraser took Anderson to his mother's for the night, and the next day drove him out of the heat of London to Glasgow. Anderson remained free for seven or eight months.

Biggs and Flower moved on smartly in order to limit the number of people who knew of their whereabouts. After a few temporary accommodations, including a stay in a flat in a high-rise block in south London, where Freddie Foreman says his sister-in-law cooked and cleaned for them, they were taken to London Bridge and hidden in the hold of a freighter destined for Antwerp, where a yellow DAF drove them to Paris for plastic surgery.

Flower was picked up in Australia in October 1969, but Biggs had already moved on. By the time he was discovered, a whole string of circumstances had made his life into a media circus. Ever hopeful, the officers in the mailroom at Wandsworth had kept his chair and unfinished mailbag waiting for him, even after they stopped sewing bags for the Post Office.

The previous three cases commanded headlines. But for each that does, there are many others that are buried or lost for one reason or another (including attempts that do not quite succeed). Which is not to say that those involved are not grateful, for having your face in the public eye is not exactly helpful when you are trying to become invisible.

Whilst Wilson and Biggs gained notoriety for their escapes, other Great Train Robbers also made attempts. One such was made by **Tommy Wisbey** and **Bobby Welch**, along with **Joey Martin** and six others at Leicester Prison in 1968. It involved the construction of a ladder that could be slotted together. Because the inmates were not able to measure the distance between the walls, they joked with the warders as to what they divined as the distance, saying they were having a bet. It appears the warders even paced out the distance for them, though it turned out to be not accurate enough. The ladder was fine for the first wall, but when they tried to run it across as a bridge to the second it fell short by a few inches. By then the alarm was raised, and they were stuck at the top of the wall.

Kevin Brown was the leader of an attempt to break out of Wandsworth in 1990 by hijacking a JCB loader. Work had been going on at the prison for a few months in the spring, laying a new path in the sterile area: the piece of ground between the inner fence and the perimeter wall where no inmate is allowed to set foot, where the dogs patrol. As a result there was a civilian presence and equipment being brought in on a daily basis. One such piece of equipment was a JCB. The idea was to hijack the vehicle and take it straight through the wall. The ideal time would have been during exercise period, when the refuse party came through to collect the bins from the mailbag shop, requiring the gate to be opened. "The plan needed plenty of bottle and a bit of luck for it to succeed," as Razor Smith wrote in his autobiography.

On 29 June, during morning break, as the gate was opened to let the trolley through, a group of five prisoners in the exercise yard pulled masks made from the sleeves of sweatshirts over their heads and headed for the three officers on the gate, took them down, and went charging through the sterile area to reach the JCB before the alarm was raised. With a yard full of cheering prisoners, the guards protecting the civilian workers turned and fled. The civilians were petrified and froze, until two of the escapees picked up shovels and threatened them, causing them to flee too. Only the driver was left in his JCB. Two escapees jumped onto the vehicle, dragged him out and sent him on his way.

The gate was locked again and officers came running through the sterile area, batons drawn. One of the escapees was in the JCB seat, trying to disengage the hydraulic legs; the others on the vehicle, armed with shovels, swung them at the officers who tried to clamber on board. Everyone thought the volunteer driver knew how to handle the vehicle, but in reality he hadn't a clue. He stalled the engine. He tried again, shifted it a bit, and then it promptly stalled. An officer jumped into a dump truck and drove it between the JCB and the wall, just as the JCB started to activate and move forward. Then, once again, it stalled and the engine flooded.

Reports suggest the whole place was in a panic; the watching prisoners were exuberant one minute, saddened the next, the guards confused and frightened. The escapees couldn't be touched because of the swinging shovels, and yet they couldn't go anywhere. Then one of the warders picked up some rubble and hurled it at the JCB, smashing its window and knocking out the driver. Within seconds a torrent of concrete was flying through the air at the escapees, hitting many of them. Razor Smith likened it to a biblical stoning.

The watching prisoners turned silent as they witnessed the escapees being knocked unconscious and set upon by the guards, like a mob in for the kill, hitting and kicking the defeated men. As the escapees were dragged away, the prisoners left in the exercise yard turned to face the forty or so officers standing there. A riot was feasible. Razor Smith relates how he stepped forward and threw one punch, and then another, until he was beaten to the ground. He had thought the others would follow, but only one joined him. He was dismayed at the "big-talking wankers" who continually mouthed off about what they would do if they had the chance. "At that moment I lost faith in prisoner solidarity."

Kevin Brown, a career criminal, was part of a gang that became known as the Untouchables in 2001, because it took four retrials to resolve a charge of armed robbery. One of the trials was stopped because of information that he was about to take an officer hostage and escape. Earlier, he had made an attempt to escape from an armoured prison van when taken from Long Lartin to Winchester, resulting in a dead guard dog, an officer with a broken wrist and a wrecked prison van. In 2005 he was arrested in Sidcup High Street, after a robbery was thwarted by Flying Squad surveillance and a dramatic car chase that ended on the threshold of the local police station.

Several decades earlier, three prisoners who had watched the routine of an oil tanker delivery decided it would be their way out of Dartmoor Prison. Just after 9am on 24 June 1963, **James Jennings**, **Raymond Matthews** and **Leslie Moore**, all imprisoned for robbery, made a run from the exercise yard to the tanker as the driver was tidying up the hoses after unloading, seized the cab from him and the escorting officer and turned it round to leave. Despite stones and objects thrown at them, which shattered the windscreen, they veered past the main gate, which might have withstood a battering, and headed for an unmanned gate at the end of the football field, gaining speed as they went. The momentum carried them through the first gate, made of wood, then the second gate, made of steel.

Once they were through, they quickly sought to abandon their damaged vehicle and flagged down a passing car, hijacking it and taking off toward the town of Two Bridges. When they found the car was low on petrol they abandoned it at Soussons Common, concealed it with branches and ferns, and decided to lie low until the heat died down. However, the car had been seen in the woods, and a Territorial Army unit exercising on the moor came to help in the search, finding the escapees in the fern covering among the young fir woods.

The routine of refuse collection is another obvious weak point of prison security. At Brixton Prison in May 1973, a dozen prisoners hijacked the refuse truck, scaring away its crew by wielding table legs and other objects as bludgeons, including what looked like a gun but was in fact a bar of soap carved and blackened with shoe polish. Once aboard the truck they drove it at the iron gates, crashing through it until the arms of the truck's hopper caught and the escapees had to flee on foot. Cars were commandeered, but in their panic they collided into each other. When one group climbed into a van that had been left waiting, the driver forgot to release the handbrake, losing valuable time. All were recaptured, among them **Mickey Salmon, Bruce Brown, Danny Allpress** and **Jimmy Wilkinson**, who were awaiting trial as a result of statements given by the supergrass Bertie Smalls.

Another escape from Dartmoor began in the blacksmith's shop, when two inmates realised that a high window gave them access to a boundary wall that was barely watched over. On 8 June 1988, **David Meads** and **Terence Poole,** using oxyacetylene torches from their jobs in the workshop, laboured behind a protective screen adjacent to the window and cut the bars that overlooked the walkway between the boundary wall and the inner security fence. Taking a metal ladder through the window, they ran it up the eighteen-foot wall. It was too short so they had to jump down the other side, Meads hurting his ankle in the process.

When they were spotted making for the woods, two prison officers set off after them with a dog. The dog faltered, as it could not get over a damaged wire fence because of its angle, but one of the officers continued. Unfortunately for Meads, this officer was a marathon runner, and he soon caught up with the escapee. A thorough search for Poole drew a blank until, when making a fresh comb of the area, a dog was seen sniffing at a tree right on the edge of the woods. Up in the branches sat the other escapee. He had seen the officer and, knowing he was an athlete, thought to hide out as long as it took for the search to be abandoned.

There are escapes that one would like to know more about, but for which information is in short supply, or has to be pieced together from various sources. In the 1990s, **Steve Hostetler** made it away from the laundry at Wandsworth Prison. Despite various attempts, no one had succeeded in escaping from Wandsworth since Biggs went over the wall.

Hostetler was able to force open the shutter door to the loading bay at the laundry and scale the perimeter wall at its lowest point. Unusually, steel shutters were the way out rather than a door and a barred gate.

Along with an accomplice, Hostetler had found a disused piece of piping and set about flattening the end in a door jamb. At the same time, they had made a thirty-foot rope from bed sheets and attached it to part of a broken swivel chair to make a grapple. One afternoon, they levered the shutters with their homemade crowbar enough to slide underneath it. It took a few attempts to get the grapple to hold on the wall, but once it did they were up and over, dropping down the other side, although one twisted his ankle in the process. Nevertheless, they both made it to a local cab office and were driven off into the sunset.

Why should some cases get attention and others not? It's partly to do with the media, partly to do with political sensitivities at the time. Sometimes it's the prison staff who allow the information to spread, because it bolsters their own demands, or who, conversely, suppress the information. Thus you find that a prisoner like **Ronnie Pewter,** who escaped from the Parkhurst Special Security Unit in October 1991, was barely mentioned – even though he was only the second person to escape from this 'prison within a prison', as it was called. Long-term maximum security prisoner Charles Bronson notes that no one knows how he managed the escape: "some say he walked out disguised as a building worker, some say he climbed into the back of a lorry." Perhaps that is why it had so little publicity; it is embarrassing to lose someone from a high-security setup, and yet to not quite know how it happened.

Some are oft mentioned but rarely written about. Back in the laundry room at Wandsworth Prison, we find **Georgie Madson.** Frankie Fraser and others talk about Madson as a legendary escapee, always on the lookout to grab the opportune moment. In April 1943, when he was serving a short sentence in Wandsworth, he was with some others repairing and whitewashing the laundry room roof, perched atop a ladder, when he noticed a warder come through the gate to deliver a message and go back out, closing but not locking any of the gates. Expecting him to return to lock up, they waited. Nothing happened.

Madson and friends went down the ladder, across to the gate and, finding that it did indeed open, returned for the ladder and went over the wall. In those days, if you were free and were not caught for another offence for the remaining period of your sentence, then the slate was wiped clean, a kind of gentlemen's agreement. Two years later, so the story goes, Madson turned up at the prison with his solicitor, asking for his clothes to be returned.

Another of his escapes is notorious. On the morning of Saturday 24 June 1961, when there was a reduced staff on duty, Madson led the capture of two warders in the mailroom at Wandsworth. Whilst they were being tied up, Madson pulled on an officer's hat and brown coat and sat in his box, watching over the mailroom. Then he marched those seeking to escape (variously reported as ten men or six men) across the yard. "They had no clue how they were going to get away," one former associate recalls. All was resolved when they saw a ladder that the works people had been using. Although they grabbed it and went over the wall, "They had no help outside, nothing." (Another account says that cars were waiting outside, provided by Ronald Jeal who had been released three weeks earlier. One guy had reputedly broken his leg and had to be lain on the backseat.) As a result, half-day Saturday work was ended inside the prison.

Richard Dennick used the cover of a birthday party to aid his escape, after getting over the wall of Lewes Prison in 1983. One evening, while watching television in the TV room, Dennick, who was serving life for murder, noticed some decorators' scaffolding and thought he could gain access to the roof that way. He returned to his cell to collect a few things and, remembering *The Great Escape*, stuffed some sheets into a pair of jeans and left it looking like a dummy on his bunk. Back in the TV room, he waited until everyone had gone off to bed. Three cleaners were still lurking around, but, as soon as he jumped up the scaffolding, they turned a blind eye and quickly left the room. When the guard came in to check, he only saw an empty room and locked it up for the night. Dennick was still on top of the scaffolding and had until morning to leave.

Finding the plasterboard between the rafters, he scraped it away with a scaffold clip, making a hole big enough to get into the cavity, and then prised away the tiles until he could get onto the roof. He tied the TV cable he had ripped out to a drainpipe and abseiled down the forty-five-foot wall. The last fifteen feet were quicker, as the cable snapped and he plummeted, landing on his arse and breaking his front teeth.

After crossing the yard, he threw his blanket over the razor-wire fence and went over. The wire cut his chin to the bone, but he ignored it. Though he was spotted by a guard and his dog, and the alarm was raised, he kept running. He changed his clothes in a back garden and tried to walk down the road normally. That is when he heard loud music coming from a club and went inside. It was almost closing time, but he was bought a drink by one of the partying crowd. Dennick decided to confide in the birthday boy, who didn't shirk but suggested he join them on a coach taking them into the coastal Sussex town of Brighton.

Dennick went his own way once they were in the seaside town, calling some friends who brought him clothes and money. (They tossed the bundle of clothes out of the car at an arranged spot, as they refused to be involved any further.) He checked into the Metropole hotel, drank from the mini-bar and paid his bill the next day, before leaving for London. After meeting up with some new accomplices, they robbed a corner shop of £250. They were arrested almost immediately. Dennick was later located in Wormwood Scrubs, charged with possession of a firearm under another name.

In the USA, **Richard Lee McNair** has escaped from prison three times in the last twenty years, the most recent instance being in April 2006, from the US Penitentiary in Pollock, Louisiana. This was the one to draw him to public attention, for he was captured on camera by a patrolman who stopped him down the road by a railroad track, along which he was jogging. The episode, which lasts ten minutes, was filmed by a camera in the patrolman's car and can be viewed online. It shows McNair calmly handling the officer, joking about the escapee, even giving him two different names within that short space of time. Despite fitting the escapee's profile, we see McNair finally shaking hands with the officer and trotting off on his way.

McNair was finally caught in October 2007, by the Royal Canadian Mounted Police in New Brunswick. He escaped from the maximum-security prison by burying himself under the mailbags, as he was employed in the workshop mending damaged sacks. He had built a case on a mail pallet to hide in, which was then taken out to a nearby unguarded warehouse. You could say that he mailed himself out of prison. In fact, he was the first person in thirteen years to escape successfully from such a high-security institution. Previously he had been in the super-maximum security prison at Florence, Colorado, from which no one had ever escaped. Realising he would not be the first, he had actively sought a transfer to Pollock.

Lucien Rivard, the Canadian mobster and drug trafficker, was imprisoned in Montréal's Bordeaux Prison, awaiting extradition to the United States. In March 1965, along with his companion André Durocher, he asked the guard if they could go to the furnace room to collect the hoses to water the outdoor rink – on an above-zero evening when the water would not freeze! Subsequently, Durocher pulled a gun – which was, in fact, carved wood blackened with shoe polish – and tied up the guard before restraining another guard on the west wall. They used a ladder to climb the small interior wall and the hoses to climb over the large exterior wall. Once away they hijacked a car, paying its owner a fare and later phoning to tell him where they had parked it. Durocher was picked up in a Montréal flat after a tip-off a couple of months later, and Rivard was found sunbathing at a cottage near Chateauguay with some of his associates. No escape charges were brought in order to speed up the extradition process.

Frankie Fraser gives cat burglar **Ray Jones** his vote for the best single-handed escape, when he went over the wall at Pentonville Prison, breaking both his legs in the process and yet still getting away. Fraser gives scant details, but somehow, in 1958, Jones managed to climb onto the prison roof and, in scaling down the sheer face of the outside wall, smashed one kneecap, then fell and broke his ankle. Nevertheless, he continued, scaled another wall, and broke the other leg when he jumped.

Still he persisted, crawling into a block of flats and making his way onto a roof, where he fell headlong through a skylight as he tried to prise it open. When he regained consciousness he made his way out of the building, pulled himself along using the railings on the Caledonian Road, crawled across the road to King's Cross station, over the railway lines and into someone's garden. Eventually he decided to seek help and attracted the attention of some young men, asking them to give him a lift "because I had had a bad fall." They guessed who he was, but didn't betray him. After they left him at his relative's flat, his wife arrived and arranged for him to stay elsewhere, where he remained for five months while recovering from his injuries. He was not recaptured for two years.

When **Glen Hewson** attempted to escape in 1982 from Peterhead and fell from the perimeter fence, breaking both legs, he was able to sue for damages, claiming the guards were throwing stones and bits of concrete at him. In 1987 he received £35,608, the judge being unimpressed by evidence offered by the prison officers.

I make no apologies for periodically including failed attempts, along with those that succeeded. There is sometimes a fine line between the two and, in any case, the failures still show the *modus operandi*.

Noel 'Razor' Smith mentions a couple of his failures to get over the wall of the Verne, at Portland Bill in Dorset. The way out was best pursued at night, after last roll-call at 9pm. One disadvantage of the location was that, as soon as someone went missing, the causeway was blocked and the naval police from the Royal Navy base at the bottom of Portland Bill joined in the search.

Smith mentions teaming up with Andy Philipson to scale the walls. Their first bid entailed taking a fifteen-foot piece of timber from the woodwork shop and nailing it with six-inch nails as handholds. Unfortunately, that attempt was spotted by the night patrol and they hightailed it before being caught. The next time out they went for bed-sheets tied into a rope, with a grapple attached, made from a sawn-up tubular chair. Their mistake was to not braid the rope, for it was a stormy night and the rain soaked both them and their sheets. The sentries failed to spot them in the open, as they were probably dozing, and, after two attempts to get the grapple to hold, Philipson shot up the rope and straddled the wall. But the sheet tore for the heavier Smith, who couldn't reach the dangling end to haul himself up the rest of the way. Though he threw up the broken end, Philipson hadn't the strength to hold it whilst Smith climbed. Smith told Philipson to go it alone, but he refused and dropped back down with the intention to try another night.

Reggie Kray tells the story of **Dave McAllister**, who at one time robbed the prison safe before making his escape, and another time charmed a teacher into hiding him in the boot of her car and driving him out. He had told her that, if they were caught, she was to claim that he told her a bomb was rigged in the car which he threatened to detonate. In the event, the escape was successful and he remained free for a month. But the love-struck teacher was unable to hold her tongue under questioning. She received six years for aiding and abetting him.

Francis Quinn left Frankland Prison in 1992 in the back of a laundry van. He was the first person to escape from Frankland since it opened in 1980, but there was barely any press coverage. When **Barry Redfern** and **Edward Pollock**, two loyalist prisoners, tried to repeat the method of an earlier escape from Long Kesh in 1973, by **Brendan Hughes** in a refuse collection lorry, they hadn't taken into account the modernisation of the dustcarts. The compressors set to work before they were through the gates. Both were badly injured and one died in hospital.

Joseph Steele kept escaping from prison for one reason only: to call attention to what he claimed was a miscarriage of justice, his own conviction for murder. His initial escape, in August 1989, was from custody when visiting his sick mother. He climbed through a skylight onto the roof and sat astride the ridge tiles to draw the media, photographers and local people to witness his protest. After three hours, he returned to his escort.

Four years later, in April 1993, on a similar trip home accompanied by one officer, he went out the bedroom window and, instead of hanging around Glasgow, was found five days later outside Buckingham Palace, glued to the railings. He had handcuffed his left wrist to a gate railing and superglued his right to another. A police van and ambulance were strategically parked to block him from public view. It took over an hour of solvent application before his hand was unglued.

A few weeks later Steele was on the sports field at Saughton Prison in Edinburgh, watching a game of football, when he slipped away with four others. There was only a perimeter fence topped with razor-wire at the extreme end of the outfield. Though there was a security camera, it did not cover the corner to which they fled, or the spot where a hole was already cut. Two of them were soon recaptured, but Steele telephoned the *Daily Record* and stated that he would continue his protest from abroad. More publicity was forthcoming this time. Six weeks later he turned up outside Barlinnie Jail, where he made speeches with film crews in attendance before giving himself up to the authorities.

Pearse McAuley and **Nessan Quinlivan** were two IRA members on remand in Brixton Prison, awaiting trial for conspiring to kill Sir Charles Tidbury, a Tory Party backer and brewery tycoon. Their escape occurred on Sunday 8 July 1991. On the way back to their cells after hearing mass in the prison chapel, McAuley bent down to his shoe and produced a small gun that he fired in the air before sticking it to the head of one of the guards. As Category A prisoners, they were supposed to be accompanied at all times when out of their cells.

Taking the keys, the pair opened the gates into the yard. Other warders followed, but held back as McAuley shot one in the leg. There was a wheelbarrow in the yard left by workmen. They piled it on top of a dog kennel placed against a perimeter wall and clambered up, cutting themselves on the razor-wire at the top. After dropping to the ground outside, they commandeered a prison officer's car that he was cleaning and drove off. They were immediately blocked by another guard in his car. This time they set off on foot towards Brixton Hill and hijacked another vehicle, the driver objecting and receiving a shot in the leg for his remonstration. His passenger was ejected too, and McAuley and Quinlivan sped off down the hill, abandoning the car soon after and taking a taxi to Baker Street, carrying with them a case of clothes and some money they found in the car. By the time the alarm was put into effect, they were underground, blending in with the public. As remand prisoners, they were entitled to wear their own civilian clothes.

Initially, the gun was thought to have been smuggled in via the confessional box, though it was later discovered to have entered in the sole of a training shoe when the prison metal detector was unavailable. There were also some suggestions that MI5 had allowed their escape to happen in the hope of being led to IRA safe-houses.

McAuley and Quinlivan were both recaptured in Ireland in April 1993, within days of each other. Both men carried loaded revolvers, though neither made any attempt to use them. They knew what they were doing. The Dublin courts refused to extradite them, stating that the offence of having a weapon in the Republic took precedence over any UK issues.

There have been many attempts to escape from prison by the IRA. As a self-proclaimed army, the repeated refusal to be acknowledged as such by the British authorities – who treated each offence as criminal rather than political – meant they had a virtual duty to escape. In November 1971, at Belfast's Crumlin Road Prison, nine IRA prisoners playing football abandoned their game and ran towards the prison wall as soon as two rope ladders were sent flying over. The operation to get them over the wall and into waiting cars happened so quickly that the prison officers failed to respond.

On 10 June 1981, having had guns smuggled into the Crumlin Road Prison by visitors over a period of time, eight IRA prisoners – **Joe Doherty, Robert Campbell, Angelo Fusco, Paul Magee, Michael McKee, Anthony Sloan, Gerard Sloan** and **Michael Ryan** – arranged to meet lawyers in the visiting area. After an hour, Magee, one of the leaders, produced a gun and held it to the head of a guard, prompting Doherty to follow suit. Ten officers and three solicitors were tied up; some of the prisoners changed into the guards' uniforms, whilst others disguised themselves with the solicitors' clothes and briefcases.

They made for the gates, and although they were recognised it was always at the last minute and each guard was overcome before he could take action. However, another officer some distance away thought that something was wrong and, as the prisoners were escaping through the second set of gates into the outside parking area, a gun battle ensued between the IRA backup team with cars and the police in the court opposite the jail. Only three escaped in a car, which was riddled with submachine gunfire in the process. The others made it on foot, remarkably, because for a republican to walk through the loyalist Shankhill estate was like sticking his head into a lion's mouth – though a hijacked car completed their bid to reach the safety of the Falls Road area.

'The Great Escape', as it became known, from the Maze (formerly Long Kesh), near Lisburn, outside Belfast, came as a big surprise. This prison was regarded as extremely secure, with more officers than prisoners and more sophisticated systems than most. As was later revealed, the officers' slackness resulted from the way the prisoners worked to lull them into a false sense of security. Larry Marley was to organise the escape, though he was ordered not to depart as his release was imminent.

It began at 2:30pm on 25 September 1983, a quiet Sunday afternoon worked only by a skeleton staff to reduce the overtime bill. On this day thirty-eight IRA prisoners would escape, all of whom were either housed in Block 7 or had contrived to be working there. With inmates free to move around the wings for recreation, some prisoners strategically placed themselves near officers so that they would not be able to reach the alarm buttons.

On a signal these prisoners produced guns that had been smuggled in and took control, though not without some injuries to the officers. Twenty minutes later the staff were all secured in two games rooms and their uniforms removed. The plan was to hijack the kitchen truck that visited each day at 3pm, and to conceal the mass escapees in the back. At that time they would avoid the staff shift change. But on that day the truck was late and, when it arrived, at 3:30pm, they had to turn it straight around.

The driver was an officer, but he was driving with his foot tied to the clutch and an inmate lying on the floor, with a gun trained on his crotch. All went without incident through the first two gates, but when they finally reached the main gate the next shift of officers was arriving in greater numbers. Nine of the prisoners who had changed into uniforms jumped from the back and took control of five officers in their lodge, then rounded up more guards as they entered. At one point an alarm was triggered, but when the control room checked they were informed it was a mistake.

The escape started to falter when a guard tried to break free. He was stabbed and died later. That incident was enough to send out serious alarm signals. One officer contacted the emergency control, another watchtower guard phoned to say he could see officers fighting. In the resulting fracas, everyone had to make a break for it, fleeing on foot as the gate opened.

Outside, rolls of perimeter wire trapped some of the escapees, while others managed to negotiate it. Troops and police by the hundred flooded the area. Of the thirty-eight who escaped, nineteen were caught immediately or soon after, and nineteen got away – though in the long term, only three were never recaptured: **Séamus Campbell**, **Tony McAllister** and **Gerard Fryers**. This was the biggest escape in British history, and the biggest in Europe since World War Two.

A similar operation, though on a smaller scale, occurred in the United States. The escape of the 'Texas Seven' – **Joseph Garcia, Randy Halprin, Larry Harper, Donald Newbury, Patrick Murphy Jr., George Rivas** and **Michael Rodriguez** – in December 2000 has been likened to a commando escape in the best war-movie tradition, because the planning was meticulous and came to fruition over almost two hours without detection. It happened in the John Connally Unit near the city of Kenedy. Six were captured a month later; the seventh killed himself rather than be arrested. All had been convicted on various charges of armed robbery and murder.

13 December was an ice-cold day. A number of those bent on escape, led by Rivas, asked if they could stay back and take their lunchbreak in the maintenance department, where they were waxing the floor. One of the supervisors said he would stay with them, whilst the others went for lunch. Rodriguez, who had been in the law library, managed to convince the guards to let him into that area on the pretence of collecting rubbish. He remained seated outside the department as a lookout.

Rivas came to fetch the supervisor in his office at 11:30am, and took him into the warehouse on the pretext of asking a question about the machinery, whereupon he attacked the supervisor with an axe handle. They took his clothes, sunglasses, keys and wallet with credit cards and cash, then bound and gagged him and put him in the electrical room. With the keys they obtained access to pliers, hacksaw blades and bolt cutters. When two others came back from lunch they were engaged in conversation and then grabbed. Gathering more clothes, keys and identification cards, they bound them and took them to the electrical room, then did the same with two others returning from lunch – drawn into the warehouse, captured, their clothes removed, locked up – and then three others.

At 12:40am another supervisor returned, this time with two inmates who were not in on the escape. Nevertheless, they were added to the growing numbers who were bound and gagged. This happened two more times with returning supervisors. Once the escape team were satisfied that everyone had returned, they secured the electrical room door. By then a maintenance truck had been brought into the shop area, and a cardboard and plywood shelter that had been made earlier was placed in the back of the truck to hide the escapees for the ride into town.

Prison Break

At 1:05pm they received a phone call from a supervisor for a headcount. With one of their number impersonating an officer, they kept their cool and responded correctly. This was an operation that had to work systematically, relying on accurate planning. They were not surprised when they could hear noise from the electrical room, as those inside were managing to free themselves. But it was too risky to go in to silence them, so they bound the door tighter with cable. An alarm was eventually triggered from inside the electrical room, but the control room believed it to be a fault and silenced it. All in all, nine civilian maintenance supervisors, four prison officers and three non-participating inmates were held in the electrical room.

The next stage was to phone and inform the back gate that maintenance men would be coming into the area that led to the back gate and perimeter road to install video monitors. It sounded authentic, for similar work had been carried out elsewhere.

A gator – similar to a golf cart – bearing two of the men in civilian clothes and two disguised as workers went to the back gate. They entered the gatehouse and received a call from the maintenance department to ask if they had arrived yet. As a result, no identification was sought. Caught unaware, the guard was captured, bound, gagged and placed in the adjoining restroom. This procedure was repeated at the exterior gate by entering the tower and disarming the guard, first with a call from the maintenance department to lull him into laxity. After showing them where the guns were stored, he too was bound and gagged.

With their position secured, Randy Halprin phoned the maintenance department and told the others to leave. When the white truck arrived, they climbed in with their armoury and all seven drove out of the prison. One of the notes they left behind quoted a line from the Kris Kristofferson song, 'Me & Bobby McGee': "Freedom's just another word for nothin' left to lose." It wasn't long before one guard broke free and raised the alarm, but it was too late. The abandoned truck was found at 4pm at a Wal-Mart store in Kenedy. The seven staged a handful of robberies, killing a policeman during one, before eventually being recaptured. All are now on death row awaiting execution.

Martin Gurule managed to evade death row at Texas' Huntsville Prison by deception. In December 1998, along with six other prisoners, he padded his bunk with pillows to make it appear as if he were asleep, whilst in reality he had stayed outside in the exercise yard. There they all cut through a fence and climbed onto a roof to wait until after midnight, when they could make their bid. They had planned this for some while, using felt pens to colour their prison overalls a camouflaged grey. But their move towards the perimeter fence was spotted as they came down from the chapel roof. Though the guard fired, freezing six of them in their tracks, Gurule kept going and managed to scale two ten-foot fences with razor-studded tops, escaping into the woods.

The area was notorious for its snake-infested swamps. He was discovered a week later, drowned in a creek a mile from the prison, by two off-duty officers out fishing. Why he had not been found earlier in such an obvious place provoked questions, particularly as a massive hunt had drawn a blank. Gurule was the first person in sixty years to escape from a Texan death row, the previous case being that of **Raymond Hamilton**, an associate of Bonnie and Clyde in the 1930s.

For many years the gallows was kept in storage for **Terrible Tommy O'Connor**, an armed robber and cop killer who gained his stay of execution by escaping from his Chicago prison cell just three days before he was scheduled to hang. This occurred in December 1921, when O'Connor feigned illness and was removed from his cell to the hospital. There he drew a gun on his warders that had been smuggled in and delivered to him by the prison's cook.

With four others he scaled the walls and hijacked a car. He was never seen again.

When the mode of execution was changed in 1928 to the electric chair, as O'Connor had been sentenced to hang, the gallows was disassembled and stored – though not totally dismantled until 1977, by which time they determined he would probably not be coming back. He would have been in his early nineties by this time. At that point the gallows was placed in storage in the basement of the Chicago Criminal Courts Building, and later sold to a Wild West museum in Union, Illinois.

So where did O'Connor go? Some say Ireland, whilst others were sure that he became a monk. A Broadway play that drew on his story, *The Front Page*, was staged in 1928, inspiring three films in turn – *The Front Page* (1931 and 1974), *His Girl Friday* (1940) and *Switching Channels* (1988) – showing how much his case held prominence with the public at the time.

The famous Sing Sing Prison at Ossining, which is up the Hudson river, north of New York City, is a prison with a formidable record for failed escape attempts. But on 13 April 1941, **Joseph Riordan, Charles McGale** and **John Waters** started their escape bid from the hospital on the third floor. A year in the planning, Riordan had gained a bed in the hospital with symptoms for appendicitis and McGale with a sprained back, whilst Waters worked there as an orderly. All three had convictions for armed robbery.

But no matter how well you plan the inside part, as we have seen, once outside one has to be equally rigorous.

It all started a year earlier, when Waters had wondered about the milk truck that made daily deliveries. He asked a friend on the outside to track its course, and then devised a plot to package three guns and three sets of handcuffs and strap them to the underside of the truck at the loading platform in Newburgh. Thus, when the truck arrived in Sing Sing, McGale, who was a trusty, would remove the package. They had already prepared keys that unlocked doors from the cellar to a utility tunnel of steam pipes that led through to the central railroad tracks outside the prison. They had been down the tunnel and prepared the way by sawing through an iron plate and replacing it loosely.

Thus, around 2am, as their guard made a tour of the hospital, he was ambushed and left with two bullets in his body. (The guard wasn't the only one to die. Another inmate had a heart attack as he watched.) The shots did not awaken many, but they did find a trusty in the corridor and another guard, both taken hostage and marched down to the basement, where they were bound. After they had gone through the tunnel and the iron plate, they used a rope they had planted earlier to drop the thirty feet to the railway tracks, and then went to meet their accomplices a couple of hundred yards away in the station plaza.

Their friends were supposed to be waiting with a car. However, things had gone too smoothly and they arrived earlier than expected, going off to a bar to kill time. All the escapees found was the getaway car, a 1939 Plymouth sedan, with a submachine gun sitting on its backseat, parked and waiting but without its driver.

They also encountered two policemen on routine patrol, who saw the three men wandering around in search of their friends. They were challenged, and it quickly developed into a shootout with one policeman and one escapee, Waters, shot and killed. Riordan and McGale fled, and their two getaway accomplices, suddenly stranded, tried to take a cab but were themselves arrested. Riodan and McGale got away, forcing a shad fisherman to take them across the Hudson to the Rockland County side. Bloodhounds located them within a few hours in the woods, and they surrendered their guns without a fight.

Prison Break

San Quentin, like many a state prison, has had its fair share of breakouts throughout its history. However, this particular prison has witnessed two mass escapes that are historically interesting in that they both involve taking the governor hostage.

On 22 July 1862, ten inmates broke line and made a run for the main gate to reach the warden's office. They grabbed the governor and, holding him hostage, made their way out of the camp. In the *mêlée*, upwards of three hundred inmates took advantage of the situation and grabbed whatever they could as weapons to escape from the compound. The main group found that the governor was a bulkier character than they had expected, and he soon became exhausted and collapsed. They had to abandon him, leaving themselves at the mercy of the guards on horseback in pursuit. Many were shot and killed that day. Few escaped for good.

Just over seventy years later, on 16 January 1935, a meeting of the prison board was disturbed when four armed inmates entered the room (their guns smuggled in under the dashboard of an unknowing civilian employee) and took the governor and others hostage. They commandeered the warden's car to make their escape, but were eventually halted when a police roadblock shot out their tyres. A gun battle followed in which the leader, **Rudolf Straight**, was killed, though none of the hostages were badly injured.

There were strong suggestions following this escape that the police should not be afraid to shoot at escapees, even if the hostage was a prison governor – the argument being that it was a self-inflicted fate, since "the keeper who cannot keep himself out of their hands is no great shakes and ought not to be spared," as the local Sacramento newspaper commented.

Henry Williams went over the wall of London's Newgate Prison in an almost impossible sense, in 1836. Condemned for burglary and waiting to be executed, his cell led to an adjoining courtyard where he could go freely to exercise, for it was surrounded by a fifty-foot granite wall. No one was expected to escape from there. It was much like a zoo cage with an outdoor airing space. But then no one appeared to have had a clue about Williams' background. As a child he had been a sweep's boy, his skill being to climb up inside a chimney. He had left that occupation one day when he climbed up inside a forty-foot sugar refinery chimney and went out over the top, climbing down to a new life outside.

The airing yard at Newgate offered a problem to anyone who might think to escape, as the granite stone was smooth and cold. Williams chose a corner and, using his arms behind his back, worked his way upwards, moving his bare feet "like claws on the other side of the wall-angle", as *The Newgate Chronicles* noted. If he had reduced his pressure he would have fallen to a certain death. He had chosen the corner where a water cistern had been built so that he could catch hold at the top, bracing himself in the same angle, managing to grab the tank and pull himself up.

The next problem, just beneath the top of the wall, was a revolving *chevaux de frise* (iron spikes set in timber), which were razor-sharp and couldn't be grabbed to reach the top. They were also close enough to make it impossible to get between them and the wall. There was an iron rail that ran beneath the *chevaux de frise* which supported it, but it contained sharpened spikes.

Though the spikes cut into his hand, Williams held on and worked his way around the three sides of the yard, dangling from the rail until he came to a point nine feet above the flat roof of the condemned cells. Launching himself forwards into the air, he fell and clutched at the roof's ledge, clambering up onto it and working his way from building to building, jumping the gaps until he passed out of the gaol and was above the houses of Newgate Street. Wearing only his shirt and trousers, covered in blood,

Williams came across a woman hanging out her washing. He hid behind a chimney, then followed her down the attic ladder, calmed her and explained his situation. She helped him on his way, for there was a mood among the people that hanging should be for murderers, not burglars.

In her autobiography, **Zoe Progl** – the 'Queen of the Underworld' as she liked to present herself – tells of **Jumbo Parsons** and his escape from Wormwood Scrubs on 18 September 1957, to "display his resentment" at being convicted of a robbery he claimed he had nothing to do with. On that day, he was part of a team repairing the roof of the main building. When the others returned to their cells they discovered he was missing. He had hidden behind a chimney and then clambered over rooftops and down a drainpipe, before taking hold of a rope with one end tied to a tree outside the prison and managing to haul himself up the thirty-foot wall. He was driven away by friends, leaving a letter for the governor: "Dear Sir, I have enjoyed my stay in your prison and have no complaints to make about my treatment. In fact, my only complaint is that I had to leave in such a hurry, I had no time to say 'Goodbye'." It would be a month before he was recaptured.

For his next attempt, his friend Zoe, who had been asked to organise it, lined up a stolen Jaguar and waited outside the wall with three accomplices. On 15 March 1958 at 6.30am, a rope was tied to the tree for him to climb. However, when it came to it he couldn't make the final few feet, as he couldn't grip the rope near enough to the top. He admitted defeat and they returned home.

On the morning radio news it was announced that Parsons was missing, but that he might still be in the prison grounds. That evening Progl and her friends returned to check the walls, to see if he was coming over. At one point, she and a female friend were approached by two policemen, and had to spin a yarn about escaping from two men who had assaulted them when taking them home. There was still no sign of Parsons. They went away and came back at 2:15am, and again at 4am. This time they saw him climbing down the scaffolding of the gateman's lodge, and stealing a bicycle that was leaning against the wall. Progl followed, and Parsons exchanged the bike for a seat in her car. Parsons had spent much of his day hiding down a manhole in the grounds. He was motivated entirely by his case. The lawyer and the Member of Parliament he found to fight his corner convinced him to return to prison as the best way to serve his claim. Eighteen days later, he rang the bell at the gates and said, "Good evening, I've come back." Though the Home Secretary did review his case, the conviction stood.

Zoe Progl herself was the first woman to break out of Holloway Prison. Knowing that she was going to be convicted again for burglary, she set in motion plans for her escape even before the trial. Her friends thought she would do better to jump bail in the first place, and it seems strange that she did not take their advice.

Progl made a reconnaissance of the prison walls late one night, accompanied by a boyfriend and a black poodle, decoys for her presence. She measured the wall with a metal tape and found what looked like a little-used exit, a small green door. She went in search of a good locksmith and returned a few days later with a set of keys, one of which was almost certain to work. It was raining, so there was less chance of being seen whilst they went through the keys until the gate opened. To her dismay, one foot inside the gate was a double-locked door that would not relent.

Deciding the wall was her only option, she chose a section that came down in a private road beside a bombsite, ideal for disposing of a ladder that would not be found for a few hours. From the way she writes about her escape, it seems that she was determined to be the first woman to break out for, as noted, she could have merely broken her bail and avoided any further dramatics. Once she was sentenced and incarcerated she played the goody – which surprised some of the officers, who had housed her at their particular 'hotel' three times before. Fortunately, she was held in the block nearest the point in the wall that she wanted to go over. Within a few weeks she was made a trusty and given the chore of cleaning the senior medical officer's room, where she discovered by chance that one of the phones had a direct line out. Her first call made her boyfriend think she was already out, as it was in an age when a prisoner using telephones was not a standard occurrence. In the following days it became her means to communicate her plans.

On 24 July 1964, just after 7:30am, she calculated that she had a five-minute slot after being let out of the hospital by the sister, her patient-feeding duties completed, in which to cross the quadrangle and be let back into her cellblock for breakfast. An unplanned event occurred when the sister asked her to take a pint of milk over for a pregnant girl. She recounts that she dashed across to the block, left the milk by the door and shot back to the wall, clambering up a five-foot pile of coke and grabbing the top of the seven-foot inner wall.

For a few moments, there was no sign. Then she heard a metal ladder crashing against the outer wall and saw her boyfriend's head appear with a rope ladder. She had to hurry once she reached the top of the twenty-five-foot wall, for one of her girlfriends, who had come along with another woman, was having a fracas with two officers a hundred yards down the street. They thought it would be fun to watch her escape and had turned up in dark glasses, sitting in a pink Ford Zephyr with leopard-skin seat covers, parked right in front of the main gate, where officers coming on and off duty regarded them with suspicion. And this early on a Sunday morning!

Paul Buck

Progl and her boyfriend went off across the bombsite to the waiting car, joined seconds later by their friends.

Progl lay low for a week, changing her hair from blonde to red. Then, reunited with her baby daughter of two and a half, she went on the run to a caravan site near Paignton, the same place where Jumbo Parsons had fled to. For a fortnight she devoted herself to being a mother. It didn't last. She returned to London to resume her usual lifestyle and, after forty days of freedom, she was picked up when a policeman whose hobby was collecting car numbers noticed 1958 number plates on her new, stolen 1959 Consul.

The occurrences of women escaping from prison are minimal, precisely for the point Progl reveals: children and family. It is not easy to be on the run with children and their needs, nor is it easy to have to abandon them to the care of others. At that time though, Progl had taken the latter choice, a son from a previous relationship having been given up for her mother to raise.

VII
Into the Blue Beyond

An escape by air has to be organised by those on the outside. Of course, the history of such escapes does not go back too far. The use of a hot air balloon may well feature in cinematic adventures, but the reality would hardly offer a speedy departure. It is surprising, though, that helicopter escapes do not feature more heavily, for there is far less traffic in the sky than on the ground. The only disadvantage is that those below can clearly see and hear the whirling machine, and thus follow the trajectory of the escape, running the risk that faster helicopters, or even planes, can take off from nearby airports or other bases to intercept them. But the helicopter is a good means for hoisting inmates from prisons, provided it comes back to ground within a reasonable time, transferring the escapees to more conventional transport before they vanish.

There has only been one escape by helicopter on mainland Britain, and it was a long time in coming. Not only had it been predicted as far back as 1966, when prisoners protesting on the roof at Leicester Prison were buzzed by a press helicopter, but, just a couple of years later, the governor of Parkhurst had made a low-level run over his own prison and noted how easy it would be to escape that way. Even after worldwide press attention had been given to Michel Vaujour's 1986 Paris escape (noted below), there were still no precautionary measures using netting or wire in the UK.

Thus it should have been no surprise when, on 10 December 1987, Andrew Russell (using the name Andrew Downes) hired a Bell 206 Longranger helicopter from Stansted Airport. On the pretext of flying towards Market Harborough, he stuck a gun to the head of the pilot at the last moment and told him to go to Gartree Prison, in nearby Leicestershire, to touch down on the football field and collect two prisoners.

Russell and his accomplice had made a dummy run eight days earlier. That time they had landed on a golf course in the area, his pretence being that he worked for a security company and was checking out possible hijack points. From there the pair had accepted a lift from a golf club member, who saved them the trouble of calling for a taxi and took them into the town, where they visited the library to consult local Ordnance Survey maps. They asked to photocopy them, but declined to do so when asked to become members of the library. (Why hadn't they visited Stanford's, or a similar travel bookshop in London, and bought the appropriate map?) It had also been noted that they were carrying a radio frequency scanner used to monitor police signals.

On the day of the escape itself, as they came into land on the prison football pitch, two robbers on afternoon break from the workshops, **John Kendall** and **Sydney Draper**, started running towards the centre circle, waving towels as identification. Guards who tried to follow were hindered by other inmates. At 3:17pm, only twenty-one seconds after it had landed, the helicopter commandeered by Russell was lifting away from the prison with its two escapees.

The plan had been to come down on the golf course, where a getaway car was waiting with a driver. But there was a swirling mist across the course, and it couldn't be seen from the air. That plan was aborted and the helicopter touched down on an industrial estate, where the pilot was left handcuffed to his plane and the three occupants set about hijacking a delivery van. The receipt for the hire of the helicopter, still in its envelope and bearing Russell's prints, was left behind in the cockpit.

The prison had feared this might happen one day. For such an eventuality, they had instigated a plan called Operation Rogue Elephant with RAF Wittering, whereby Harrier jump-jets would scramble and intercept any helicopter. But on this December day, when an emergency call was made to the air-control centre at RAF West Drayton, the only response was an operator with no idea of the plan, or even of the existence of a place called HMP Gartree. He suggested they call the local police who, even if they had responded quickly, would still have been hard-pressed to locate the helicopter, as it was soon back on the ground.

Kendall went with Russell when they hijacked a Fiat, leaving its female driver with the delivery van. From there they went to Corby and kidnapped an old man driving a Mini Metro in a multi-storey car park, taking him along, tied up in the back, as they sped north-bound up the M1. They abandoned him in Sheffield, where he was found that evening, bound and gagged, with £40 stuffed in his pocket for the trouble they had caused him.

On the last day of January, Kendall was located in a one-room flat along Chelsea's King's Road. A forty-strong team of police with searchlights and weapons led a full assault on the building at 3am, smashing their way into the place and terrifying the neighbourhood. Kendall was asleep in bed. Unluckily for Russell, he was also there.

Sydney Draper went another way after the helicopter had come to ground. It was fourteen months before he was recaptured, in February 1989, at a house in his old stomping ground of Enfield.

Reggie Kray, who was at Gartree at the time, noted the commotion and its aftermath, particularly the witty notices on the board: "Helicopter trips/To and fro/Leicester to London. All enquiries to: Chief Security Officer." "Please check your luggage before helicopter flight." "Helicopter trips all full for the season. Check for vacancies at a later date."

One of the government's proposed methods for prevention was rocket defence, but that had to be scrapped as it was almost certain that, in any helicopter escape, the pilot would be an unwitting outsider. Barrage balloons, nets and wire barriers across exercise yards and open areas within the walls were other cited possibilities. Kray wrote that at Gartree, "they brought in anti-escape devices, including orange-coloured balls stretched across the field. From a distance they looked quite pretty, especially when the arc-lights were flickering on them."

Kendall and Draper made their way into the annals of crime history. It could just as easily have happened earlier, as Ronnie Biggs and others had been entertaining the idea of a helicopter escape from Wandsworth in the spring of 1965. However, "the police might take pot-shots at us, which didn't thrill me," confided Biggs.

Others have undoubtedly explored that same avenue. In Northern Ireland, when the possibility had come up at Long Kesh, it was discarded because the prison was too close to a British army base, and they would have alerted helicopters which were much swifter than the civilian variety.

But it was in Ireland that the first non-mainland helicopter escape happened. At Halloween 1973, an Alouette 2 hired ostensibly for aerial photography purposes by someone impersonating an American was hijacked in a field near Stradbelly by a hooded man. The next time it landed was in the exercise yard of Dublin's Mountjoy Prison at 3:40pm.

It was behind schedule. The game of football in progress as a distraction had lost its edge, and the spectators had dwindled. **Kevin Mallon** semaphored the helicopter down using pieces of white cloth, and other inmates were ready to restrain any officers. Mallon and two other important IRA prisoners, **J. B. O'Hagan** and **Seamus Twomey** (who the year before, as Chief of Staff of the Provisionals, had been in London negotiating with the British government), were lifted away. Though the officers were restrained with difficulty, they could hardly do anything as the blades were creating a dust storm. The narrowness of the yard left little room between the rotating blades and the perimeter wall, making it difficult to counteract the turbulence as the pilot struggled to take off.

The flight was short, barely six minutes to Baldoyle racecourse, where a car was to collect them. The people designated to steal the getaway car couldn't find one, and had hired a taxi instead, which they proceeded to hijack brandishing a hefty Colt .45. When the escapees climbed out of the helicopter, the getaway car was not waiting. Believing they were under surveillance, the hijackers had taken the taxi for a quick tour around the area to kill time, delaying their arrival. Once collected, the three IRA men were driven to three different safe houses and the taxi abandoned. (The taxi driver, like the helicopter pilot, was paid a full fare.)

After the escape a prison officer apparently apologised to the governor, saying he "thought it was the new Minister for Defence [Paddy Donegan] arriving" – only for a republican prisoner to retort, "it was our Minister of Defence leaving." The escape entered republican folklore, immortalised further by the Wolfe Tones in 'The Helicopter Song'.

Over the English Channel there have been a number of notable cases (each with their own twist) that have made headlines. None more so than that of **Michel Vaujour**, rescued by his wife at the time, Nadine, who took lessons to learn to fly a helicopter. Little did her instructors know that this single mother, raising her two children, was seeking to free her husband from La Santé Prison in Paris.

Vaujour had escaped three times before, but this fourth escape was to seal his notoriety. On 26 May 1986, Vaujour, serving twenty-eight years for robbery and attempted murder, made his way onto the roof of the prison, armed with a fake gun and nectarines painted to look like grenades, where he was snatched away by his wife in a hired helicopter. They landed nearby on a football pitch, where a car was waiting for them.

Vaujour was captured later in the year, when he was shot in a failed bank robbery. (Nadine had earlier been arrested at a villa in Southwest France.) The bullet hit him in the head and put him into a long coma, with profound effects upon his behaviour. In prison he had to be helped to learn to speak again.

The case had its place in history cemented by the film *La Fille de l'Air*, starring Beatrice Dalle as Nadine. As the film shows, flying over Paris – or indeed, over any major city where the airspace needs to be vigorously controlled – soon draws the authorities onto your tail.

Pascal Payet seems to have determined that his notoriety was best served by a series of helicopter escapes. Payet was serving thirty years for a murder committed during a 1997 robbery, in which he shot a security guard fourteen times with a Russian AK47 automatic assault rifle – acquiring the nickname 'Kalashnikov Pat'. In 2001,

Payet escaped from Luynes prison in the South of France with a hijacked helicopter; then two years later, while still on the run, he organised an escape for some of his comrades (**Franck Perletto**, **Eric Alboreo** and **Michel Valero)** from the same Luynes prison, using a hijacked helicopter. Though he was later captured, as were the other three men, he escaped once more in July 2007 – this time from Grasse prison, once again by a helicopter, which had been hijacked at Cannes-Mandelieu airport.

The last escape had a special touch because it took place on Bastille Day, the French national holiday that commemorates the storming of the Bastille Prison in 1789. The four men who had hijacked the Squirrel helicopter in Cannes ordered the pilot north to Grasse, where they landed on the roof of the prison at the start of the night shift. Three of them broke open the doors, threatening the guards with machine pistols and sawn-off shotguns. They knew exactly where they were going, forcing their way through a number of doors into the isolation section until they reached Payet in his cell. Within five minutes they were back on the roof and away. As with Charlie Wilson, Payet's rescuers came in to collect him – remarkably enough, for in this case everyone must have heard and watched the escape.

They touched down at a heliport next to a hospital in Brignoles, twenty-five miles inland from Toulon, not far from Marseilles, Payet's hometown. It was unusual for a helicopter to be so long in the air. But the escapee's freedom was short-lived. In September he was recaptured in Spain, not far from Barcelona. Even though he had undergone plastic surgery, he was still recognised by the Spanish police.

In July 2005, Payet was in prison at Villefrance-sur-Saone in Southern France when another attempt at rescue by helicopter failed, though this time he was not the intended escapee. Earlier, in

May 2001 at Fresnes Prison, south of Paris, a helicopter had dropped a pistol and a Kalashnikov into the exercise yard. Though two prisoners took three guards hostage, they failed to escape and were forced to surrender after twenty-four hours. Another failed attempt occurred near Lyons in 2000, when a hijacked helicopter lowered a net over the prison for three inmates on the roof to grab. Guards opened fire from a watchtower and killed one, while the other two escaped and hijacked cars once they were set down. They were later captured after a gun battle with police.

Though cables or nets were strung across some prison yards after Michel Vaujour's escape, not all took such basic preventive action. Draugignan Prison had done little to hinder escape when, in March 2001, a helicopter hijacked at an airfield near St Tropez was forced to land in the courtyard. Three robbers, **Emile Forma-Sari, Jean-Philippe Lecase** and **Abdelhamid Carnous**, leapt aboard ("the whole thing was over in a flash," a guard commented). The machine was in the air for some while, travelling the extraordinary distance of sixty kilometres to the village of Auribeau-sur-Siagne, before coming down to rendezvous with the waiting getaway car.

Another success story occurred in December 2005, when two men hijacked a helicopter in Albertville as it was in the process of taking off to collect skiers in the Alps. The pilot was forced to fly to Aiton Prison and bring it down in the exercise yard. With no security mesh, three men – one serving time for drugs, one for armed robbery and the third for leading a robbery – were lifted and taken to open country near Grenoble. All in all, almost a dozen helicopter escapes have been noted in France since 1981.

Belgium saw two such escapes in 2007, including the high-profile fifth breakout of **Nordin Benallal**, the self-styled 'escape king', though it did not go according to plan. Unforeseen by him, when the prototype helicopter – hijacked from an engineering company

and piloted by one of its employees – arrived   just
before sunset on 28 October, Benallal w   e to leap
aboard. So many inmates tried to c   onto the skids
that the plane could not lift   me failed, it came
back to earth and crashed.

Benallal and his heavily ar   accomplice leapt from the
machine, grabbed two guards as hostages and forced doors to be
opened so that they could grab a Volkswagen Golf prison car
equipped with a flashing police light and escape Ittre Prison, thirty
kilometres south of Brussels, one of the most secure modern
facilities in the country. Initially jailed in 1998 for five years on
armed robbery charges, Benallal first escaped in June 2000 and was
quickly recaptured. In October he was off again for another three
months, using a fake leg injury to obtain a crutch with which he
beat guards during a transfer between jails. His third escape was
affected in January 2001, with the help of his brother, when he
swapped clothes and places with him during a prison visit. He was
caught three weeks later in a billiard hall.

His fourth escape, in 2004, saw him cut through two wire fences
before scaling a twenty-five-foot wall with a rope ladder thrown
over by an accomplice waiting with a car. It was after this escape that
he shot two policemen who tried to apprehend him, critically
injuring them and adding substantially to the accumulating years of
his jail sentence. Benallal, who is not yet thirty, now faces over fifty
years for ninety-five convictions. One has to expect that escape will
remain his central preoccupation for the foreseeable future.

Of course, his fifth escape was short-lived. The car was abandoned
three miles away in a forest, probably the original rendezvous point
for the helicopter bid. Within a day he was recaptured in
neighbouring Holland, cornered in a motorcycle showroom. One
Belgian commentator likened his escape, the first ever from 'Belgium's

Alcatraz', to an episode of *Prison Break*. But people in Belgium want his prison to be made secure, as it also holds Marc Dutroux, the paedophile jailed for murdering four girls.

Benallal's was the second successful helicopter escape of 2007. The first took place on 15 April on the other side of the country, at Lantin Prison in Sint-Truiden, near Liège, where two men posing as tourists from Marseilles hijacked a helicopter and flew into the yard to pick up Frenchman **Erik Ferdinand**, on pre-trial detention awaiting extradition to Spain where he was wanted for fraud and theft. The pilot initially refused to land in the yard as it was too small, but at gunpoint he couldn't argue. One rescuer threw teargas canisters into the crowd of exercising prisoners, while Ferdinand clambered aboard. The helicopter flew only a few hundred metres before setting down, and the three men escaped in a waiting car.

In Holland, during September 1997, a helicopter escape attempt from De Geerhorst Prison failed when the plane crashed into the ground and killed the pilot.

The potentially lethal chaos of other prisoners clambering onboard was avoided when **Vassilis Paleokostas**, serving twenty-five years for kidnapping and robbery, was sprung from Greece's maximum-security Korydallos Prison, near Athens, on the late afternoon of 6 June 2006. Flares and teargas were thrown around the helicopter to deter stowaways. Joining Paleokostas on the escape was **Alket Rizai**, an Albanian serving life for homicide. The escape was engineered by Vassilis' brother, Nikos, who had been on the run himself for some years. They flew to a nearby graveyard in Schisto, where motorcycles were waiting to take them to the port of Piraeus.

The first such Australian escape occurred in March 1999, when librarian Lucy Dudko rescheduled her tourist flight to view Sydney's Olympic site from the sky by hijacking the copter. Coaxing the pilot with a gun to make for maximum-security Silverwater Prison, she

Left: Great Train Robber Charlie Wilson, before he escaped from Winson Green Prison in 1964.

Below: The furniture van left outside Wandsworth Prison after Ronnie Biggs' escape in 1965.

Above left: Clifford Hobbs is brought home from the 'Costa del Crime' in 2007, after four years on the run.

Above right: Brian Nichols is escorted to a court hearing at Fulton County Jail in 2005, after previously escaping from the scene of a courthouse massacre.

Below left: Alfred Hinds and his wife in 1964, after he finally won his day in court.

Below right: Patsy Fleming, who escaped with Hinds from Nottingham Prison in 1955.

Above left: John McVicar in his 1965 'Wanted' photo.

Above right: Walter 'Angel Face' Probyn, after his 1964 escape from Dartmoor.

Below: IRA man Gerard Tuite, robber/hitman James Moody and fellow thief Stanley Thompson - who escaped together from Brixton in late 1980.

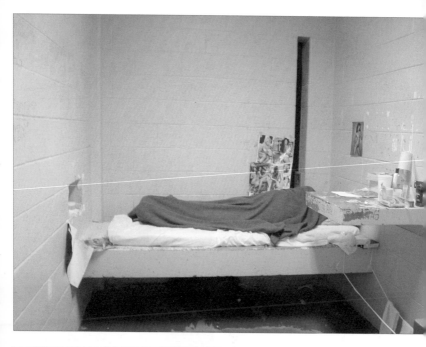

Above: Jose Espinosa's New Jersey cell, 2007. The hole he dug through to fellow escapee Otis Blunt's cell was camouflaged by pinups.

Left: A reconstruction of the Alcatraz cell of bank robber Frank Morris, who has never been located since his 1962 escape.

found her lover, **John Killick,** serving twenty-eight years for armed robbery, waiting outside in the sports area for his lift. He was whisked away to the sound of cheering inmates and a hail of bullets from the prison guards.

The helicopter landed in a park several kilometres away at North Ryde, where the pilot was tied up and the couple hijacked a car and its driver. They eluded the police for six weeks, eventually being captured at a caravan in the Bass Hill Tourist Park.

Dudko received ten years for organising the escape, and was released on parole after seven. She is allowed to write to Killick, but not to phone or visit him. His release will be in 2013 at the earliest, when he will be seventy-one and she will be fifty-five. The escape captured the public imagination, much to the annoyance of police and politicians, for being the most dramatic on record. The media gave them the 'Bonnie and Clyde' tag, or made references to the Beatles' 'Lucy in the Sky with Diamonds'. The public seemed to appreciate the romance of their exploit, and even to hope they would retain their freedom and live on the stash of accumulated earnings from earlier robberies.

Dudko had planned the escape, enquiring about hiring a helicopter earlier at Bankstown Airport, making a dummy flight a fortnight before, and buying the guns – as well as renting out three very apt films from the video shop: *The Getaway*, *Captive* and *Breakout*, in the latter of which Hollywood's Charles Bronson is hired to free an innocent man from a Mexican prison. These were all found in her flat.

In Puerto Rico, the situation of five prisoners who escaped by helicopter seemed, by our standards, worse than hopeless. **Orlando Valdes Cartagena** and **Jose A. Perez Rodriguez** were serving two hundred and fifty-four years and three hundred and nineteen years respectively for murder; **Victor Gonzalez Diaz** was serving one hundred and thirteen years, **Hector Marrero Diaz** one hundred and nine years and **Jose M. Rojas Tapia** one hundred years. It's hardly surprising that, at the very end of December 2002, two men who rented a helicopter in the capital, San Juan, ostensibly to inspect construction sites in the southern city of Ponce, forced the pilot at gunpoint to bring the helicopter down on the roof of Las Cucharas Prison where the five were waiting, having cut a hole in the chain-link fence.

One man was forced to hang onto the skids of the helicopter, as there was no room left inside, whilst they were flown into the central mountain region. All were later recaptured, except Gonzalez Diaz – whom the others claimed they killed soon after the escape, though no body was ever found. The authorities wondered if the prison's guards had played any part in the escape, for, in 1991, when the only other helicopter escape occurred, a law was brought in giving guards the authority to shoot down any helicopter during an escape attempt.

Things are pretty rough in Brazil too, where escapes happen more or less on a daily basis, and where prisons are controlled more by the inmates than the authorities. Nevertheless, a helicopter escape is a rarity. In January 2002, when a hijacked copter snatched two inmates from the central yard at the Jose Parada Neto Penitentiary in Guarulhos, a suburb of the capital Sao Paulo, guards opened fire. The machine was later found fifty kilometres away, riddled with bullet-holes. "It was fast, *Miami Vice*-style," said a military police spokesman, referring to the 1980s TV cop series.

In California, when **Ronald J. McIntosh** walked from a minimum-security prison on 28 October 1986, his purpose was to free his lover from her jail. McIntosh, who was already an experienced helicopter pilot, took a practice flight under the name Lyle Thompson with an instructor from Navajo Aviation on the

31st. On 4 November, using another alias, Fred Holbrick, he arranged to hire a machine for the next day from Aris Helicopter in San Jose.

McIntosh set off with the hire company's pilot, and forced him at gunpoint to set down at Bollinger Canyon, near Danville. He then instructed the pilot to climb out and took over the controls himself. Thirty minutes later, at 11:15am, McIntosh landed the helicopter on the prison athletic field at the Federal Correctional Institution at Pleasanton, east of San Francisco, where he collected **Samantha Lopez** who was serving a sentence for a 1981 robbery. She was waiting for him.

They were apprehended on 15 November in a Sacramento shopping mall, when they went to collect wedding rings they had ordered. The police were waiting, having monitored the bank account on which the cheque was drawn. McIntosh was subsequently given twenty-five-years for "air piracy, and using a gun in the commission of air piracy", and Lopez received a further five to add to her fifty for the bank robbery in Georgia. They appealed the conviction, claiming a 'necessity defence', which can excuse an otherwise criminal act − in this case, they claimed, Lopez had to escape because her life was in danger, as she was being threatened by prison officials, a fact they claimed the jury was not made aware of.

Lopez explained that she held a position on the Inmate Council, a group that liaised between prisoners and administration, and worked in the business office handling the prison's financial records. In her position she had pointed out various prisoners' problems to the warden, whom she claimed expressed no interest. She then made the implicit threat that people outside might be interested in "misappropriation and mismanagement of funds that she had uncovered while working in the business office", according to her attorneys. Lopez claimed that not only did the warden threaten her life, remarking that "accidents happen in prisons every day", but that from then on an increasing catalogue of other threats and actions against her were made, until she felt her only alternative to suicide was to escape. McIntosh added that he felt compelled to help her. The defence failed.

There is always the difficulty in staging a helicopter rescue of whether the machine fits into the landing space, or can lift off vertically without clipping the enclosure. It seems that the pilot who tried to aid the escape of **Benjamin Kramer** from prison in Miami misjudged his manoeuvrability and caught the blades on the wire fence, bringing the helicopter back to earth. On 18 April 1989, it swooped into the exercise yard of the Metropolitan Correctional Centre in South Dade at 10am and snatched up the waiting Kramer, a boat builder and speedboat racer serving life without much chance of parole for heading a drugs ring.

When Kramer climbed aboard he unbalanced the craft, and the pilot, probably too eager to pull away, apparently did not lift off as cleanly as he should have done. He set the helicopter in a spin, its tail hitting the concertina wire, catapulting it over the fence and causing it to crash nose-first into the prison grounds outside the exercise yard. Kramer broke his ankle, while his pilot accomplice – Charles C. Stevens, who had learnt to fly over a period of six months specifically for the escape – broke his neck. Their intention had been to transfer to a twin-engine plane that would take Kramer to Colombia.

The Metropolitan Correctional Centre is unlucky for helicopter escapees. Three years earlier, another inmate found that the contact who had arranged for him to be lifted out was in fact a federal agent. No sooner had he climbed into the cockpit than he was arrested by other agents aboard the machine.

The Chilean government were none too pleased when, at the end of December 1996, four leftwing guerrillas belonging to the Manuel Rodriguez Patriotic Front, who had fought General Pinochet's military junta, escaped from prison in a spectacular helicopter swoop. Knowing that speed was of the essence and that they would probably be engaged in a gun battle, the prisoners were to climb aboard a fisherman's basket suspended beneath the helicopter, its sides reinforced with bullet-proof vests as armour.

In the event, after the helicopter descended on the maximum-security Frente Prison in the capital, Santiago, lift-off did not go smoothly. **Patricio Ortiz** and **Mauricio Hernandez** were left clinging onto the basket. When it brought them down in a park where cars were waiting for them, Hernandez had to drop the last three metres whilst Ortiz was crushed beneath the basket and seriously injured. The third member, **Ricardo Palma Salamanca**, jumped awkwardly and found himself rolling on his head. Only the fourth, **Pablo Munoz Hoffman**, was unscathed, climbing out through the cables that had supported the basket. Ortiz later surfaced in Switzerland, seeking political asylum, and Salamanca published a book chronicling the group and its escape.

Most helicopter escapes are over in the blink of an eye, the machine coming to ground before anyone can set up chase. However, in July 1988 an aerial chase did occur after three inmates were lifted from the Penitentiary of New Mexico, near Santa Fe. The Aerospatiale Gazelle helicopter then flew eighty miles south to Mid-Valley Airport in Los Lunas, south of Albuquerque, where the police were waiting. A gun battle ensued, wounding one of the convicts, whilst another escaped on foot. The copter took off again, but this time was pursued by others, which started a battle in the skies. As one might expect to see in the movies, one of the state police helicopters was almost forced to collide with a crane, while there was an attempt to ram another pursuing craft. Eventually, low on fuel, the machine was forced down and its occupants arrested, including a woman in the cockpit.

Escape teams have also used what appear to be official helicopters. In July 1986, when a machine with state police markings attempted to lift **Stephen Vento Sr**, a known Mob figure, from the yard of the Federal Penitentiary at Lewisburg, Pennsylvania, those making the bid were armed with a grenade launcher and machineguns, an indication of the lengths to which they were prepared to go. Still they failed.

The proportion of women involved in helicopter escape bids is surprisingly high, as we have already seen. Joyce L. Bailey chartered a helicopter in December 1985, and subsequently drew a gun from her cowboy boots, forcing the pilot to land in the yard of the high-security Perry Correctional Institution, near Pelzer, South Carolina, to pick up **Jesse Glenn Smith**, **William Ballew** and **James Rodney Leonard**. The silver sedan they subsequently escaped in was left four miles from the prison. Another switch was made seven miles further, this car being abandoned in Mobile, Alabama, after it broke down. According to an investigator, Bailey had developed "a romantic attachment" to Smith, who was serving forty years for armed robbery, and had visited him in prison a number of times.

In August 1989, two women hired a helicopter in Denver on the pretence that they wanted to photograph some real estate. But, once they were nearing the Arkansas Valley Correctional Facility in Colorado, Rebecca Brown pulled a gun and directed the pilot to land in the prison yard to collect their partners, **Ralph Brown,** doing time for sexual assault, theft and criminal impersonation, and **Freddie Gonzales**, serving four years for robbery. The guards held fire because they feared the pilot was a hostage. They were flown to a waiting Ryder truck that Rebecca had kitted out with clothes, Albertson's fried chicken, Double Stuf Oreo cookies, and condoms.

They were later recaptured after a chase and shoot-out in Holdrege, Nebraska. Both Brown and Patricia Gonzales received twenty years for their venture. Today they are free, unlike their men. Rebecca has divorced and started afresh under another name. She puts her mistake down to emulating her mother's dutiful devotion to a military husband. Rebecca too thought she was obliged to stick by her man, no matter what, and so set about organising the escape that her husband had suggested.

When Rebecca herself was an inmate she was known as 'Chopper', which afforded her protection. "I would hide behind that," she admitted. "It kept me from getting beat up. I was a very weak person, but because of what I did, I had total, automatic respect." Her crime has gone down in Colorado folklore, still spoken of with awe by inmates. But she feels she has been lucky to survive both her marriage and her time in prison. "I was a doormat. I'm not that person anymore."

VIII
Forcing the Issue

It is not difficult to escape from an open prison, or any other low-security custodial institution. If you are intent on leaving then you will, whether by the front gate or over a fence. Or perhaps by going for a day out, or a weekend's home leave, and never returning.

Many more do this than might be imagined. At various times the media run scare stories on those who abscond so easily, particularly if they are regarded as 'celebrity' criminals. Others, having been imprisoned for a major crime such as murder, are often placed in low-security prisons after a relatively short time, the institution effectively dangling a carrot that may lead them to escape. There are certainly cases where escape from open prison is made for a seemingly valid reason — at least as far as the escapee is concerned.

Mary Bell joined the ranks of the infamous after killing two little boys in 1968, when she was only eleven years old. As her incarceration entered its less severe period, in 1977, she was moved to Moor Court, an open prison set among the hills of Staffordshire.

She was being prepared for the parole process, and for becoming a member of society.

Bell was not pleased. She told the governor it wasn't a "step forward", and that a less secure facility "was like being sent to prison, because you see you are *more* in prison when it's open." She was convinced she was destined to remain in prison, and that making another life outside was beyond her. Bell was twenty at the time.

The pressure to run away was great. Moor Court was like a four-star hotel set in a beautiful landscape, a millionaire's country home. It was too much for her, and for other inmates, she believed, who would have to be released eventually to high-rise flats and a more squalid way of life. "It leaves people with a feeling of discontentment, feeling they are better off in prison than outside."

'Open prison' meant what it said. She could go outside, lie on the grass, be alone. She could do anything she wanted, except go beyond the prison perimeters. As the governor explained, "What we are doing is requiring you to make your own decisions." Bell didn't know whether she could withstand the pressure of so much trust being invested in her. She warned them she would run away, that she perceived herself to be a 'lifer', and that it was all too much for her. She also demanded knockout pills. "I wanted to be blitzed."

Within three months, in September 1977, she fulfilled her own prophecy and jumped over the fence, heading off across the fields accompanied by one of her new friends, a short-timer. They went on a Sunday, once the visitors started arriving at 1:30pm. They knew that, with so many people walking around the grounds, no one would note they were missing until the next headcount at 6pm.

Once they reached the road, they hitched a lift. The first lift didn't last long, as Bell suspected the driver had twigged where they came from, as he quickly dropped them off. The next lift was from three young men, though one got out soon after. (Bell suspected he too had guessed.) The remaining two young men were heading for Blackpool, an idea that appealed to Bell and her friend. She says it wasn't long before both boys were informed where the women had absconded from, and that she was Mary Bell. One of the boys had actually read a book about her, though both swore that they would not alert anyone.

Bell later described her euphoria at riding on the big dipper, of getting roaring drunk easily, as she had no experience of drinking, and of dancing late into the night at a club. She also lost her virginity there, though she remembers little of the experience. By the second night she was back in Derby, at one of the lads' family home.

The following day, she awoke to find herself plastered over the front pages of the newspapers. The boy went to see a social worker he knew, for advice on what he should do. He returned to Bell and offered her a river barge to stay on, but she said she would head for London. Before that could happen, a motorbike policeman recognised her when she was out in the car. When he asked her to wind down the passenger window and said her name to her, despite some evasive blustering she knew the game was up. He took her to the police station.

She hoped that the 'dangerous' tag assigned to her would not stick, and that no crimes committed locally in the last few days would be attributed to her. She told the police she had intended to go to London, to work for a few months and then to give herself up, just to prove that she could do it. Her story was untrue, as she really only wanted to have a good time. But the press reported that she had left to get pregnant; the boy had succumbed to the lure of chequebook journalism, and stated that Mary wanted his baby.

She knew what awaited her though. She would soon be in another prison, "and there wouldn't be any smiling, understanding policemen, only the furious system I had kicked in the face." Two officers came from Moor Court; they told her she had been stupid, and that she had blown her chance of freedom for some years. She was taken to the less than salubrious Risley Remand Centre.

A couple of years later Mary was allocated to another open prison, at Askham Grange. By then she no longer felt the need to escape. "I no longer imagined, as I had done before, that I was a kind of prisoner, like POWs you know, who have an obligation to escape. Nor did I feel the *need* to run that I'd had at Moor Court." As she concluded, "I was ready … ready to be me again."

Mary Bell was released in 1980, to be given a new name and a new life. Her daughter, who was born in 1984, knew nothing of her mother's past until she was discovered by the media, some years later. They had to leave their home with bed-sheets over their heads. Though the daughter's anonymity was legally protected until she became eighteen, Bell took the issue to the High Court and was granted lifelong anonymity for both herself and her child.

Joe Wilkins forced the issue in an entirely different way. There are suggestions that the state had a hand in his escape in order to serve its own ends. Wilkins was a serious criminal with a long record. He was serving ten years for drug smuggling when he walked from Highpoint low-security prison in Suffolk, in 1992. Some claim he was 'sprung' by the British authorities. What is known is that he initially walked from Ford Open Prison in West Sussex, in 1991, was rearrested and moved to Highpoint. In January 1992 he was let out on day release, to travel unaccompanied to London to see his dentist. He never returned.

Wilkins departed for Spain and took up residence on the 'Costa del Crime', living in a villa in Estepona. Many believed that, for someone on the run to be living so openly, with no extradition proceedings or deportation attempted, a deal must have been struck. At the very least, the rumours ran, a blind eye had been turned in return for his help. The theory that has unravelled since, during a London money-laundering trial, is that Wilkins was employed in 1993 to introduce undercover British police into the criminal fraternities of drug and tobacco smugglers in Spain and Gibraltar, to break a laundering gang. The whole operation cost the Metropolitan Police (and thus the British taxpayer) a fortune, in the region of £25 million. After years of legal arguments the case collapsed, with the judge labelling the whole enterprise as an "illegal sting" and a "state-created crime".

Wilkins is believed to have been an MI6 and police informant on many other high-profile cases, latterly earning himself the distinction of 'supergrass' and ostracism by the British criminal fraternity in Spain.

Carrying the strong credentials of a so-called 'public enemy', **Charlie Richardson,** one half of an infamous crime partnership with his brother Eddie, walked from Spring Hill near Aylesbury, Buckinghamshire, in 1980. That year marked fourteen years served of his twenty-five-year sentence for fraud, extortion, assault and grievous bodily harm. He had been up for parole for the last seven, but was turned down each year. Once he had been moved to the open prison at Spring Hill, "I did what any self-respecting 'gang boss' would do when trusted to be moved to an open prison – I planned my escape."

Being in Spring Hill meant that Richardson was a big step closer to parole. But he no longer had the patience to wait for another year, or perhaps a further two years. Richardson had been trying to deter the guards from looking into his cell at night by screaming abuse at them. It was part of his preparations to casually leave the building under cover of darkness. He had instructed friends to meet him in the car park of a local pub at a specific time, and not to wait if he was late.

The first night, as Richardson crossed the fields, he could see the car. Time was running out, and he was just arriving when he saw the car pull away. He was obliged to retrace his steps to prison. The next night he set off earlier. Richardson arrived first this time, and was waiting as the car swept into the parking area.

He was driven straight to London, directly to Soho, as he wanted to wander around and get a feel for the place he had not seen for more than a decade – a place he now barely recognised. Then he briefly returned to his friends and family in Camberwell, before moving on to Jersey to visit a daughter in hospital, then sailing by ferry to St Malo, and from there to Paris, Nice, Majorca … where, prompted by seeing the English newspapers at this popular destination for British tourists, he thought it a better idea to move down to the Spanish mainland (even if he did eventually gravitate to Benidorm to be amongst his fellow countrymen). At one point he wrote to *The Sunday Times* about his campaign for release, and they published the letter. When he did slip back into Britain, he was quickly discovered and returned to prison. After serving another four years, Richardson was finally released in August 1984.

Whilst most prisoners know they will be released sooner or later, for **Harry Roberts** the prospect does not seem to be on the cards. Now that child-killer John Straffen has died in prison, Roberts is today the UK's longest serving prisoner. It may seem unreasonable that he should still be in prison, having been sentenced in 1966 to a minimum of thirty years for killing three policemen at Braybrook Street, Acton. It seems he was heading towards release in 1999, and was moved to Sudbury Prison in Derbyshire, perhaps in preparation. He worked unsupervised at an animal sanctuary some thirty miles from the prison, though he didn't always turn up each day. On those days he was reported to have journeyed to London, and was seen with "some very unsavoury people". When he was given five days' leave, he was also seen celebrating his sixty-fifth birthday in Sheffield with Kate Kray. He was moved back into a closed prison, accused of dealings in drugs, and it seems fairly certain he will stay in prison until he dies.

His only 'time out' has been from open prisons, but it is believed that he attempted twenty-two escapes over the years. Amongst these are a few that should be noted. Reggie Kray recalled how Roberts tunnelled deep beneath his cell in Parkhurst, going through a three-foot-thick wall, and was almost as far as the outer wall before he was discovered. They found miniature arc-lights, torches and chisels. Kray stated that Roberts used to dispose of the dirt in the garden, tucking it down his trousers and releasing it in the vegetable plot, where he had been working on a goldfish pond.

Whilst his mother was alive, so the story goes, she would bring in escape equipment for him baked into cakes, directing him not to eat a specific fairy cake because it contained a compass or a file. Another time she brought in bolt cutters stashed in her bra, intending to leave them in the toilets for him to retrieve later. It seems the haul of his accumulated equipment included a masonry drill, a metal bar, pliers, sunglasses, wire cutters, a knife, a gas lighter, maps of the Isle of Wight and £20 cash.

When he was in Leicester Prison, Roberts became friends with an IRA prisoner. They concocted a plan together to make a crossbow to fire into a nearby park, where IRA associates would attach explosives to the rope for them to haul back and blast their way out. Of course they had no elastic, so a relative of the Irishman came up with the idea of knitting a number of tank-top jumpers for Roberts and other inmates, the bottom rows made of strong elastic for them to unpick. They were discovered when their diagram of the prison and the park with the arrow's proposed trajectory, fixed behind a painting, fell from his homemade frame during security checks as it was being sent out of the prison.

Walter Probyn, undoubtedly one of the greatest escapees from the British penal system, had plans to escape with Roberts, but came to the conclusion that he "was living in a world of fantasy … the only way he could survive is the thought of escaping … He was pitting his wits against the screws to find ways, but it was only in theory – he didn't want to do it in practice."

IX
Beyond the Bounds

There have always been circumstances when prisoners are taken outside the prison to work, usually watched over by guards. One celebrated case from the late nineteenth century occurred in Scotland. **John Watson Laurie** had been imprisoned for the murder of Edwin Rose, whom he had robbed and murdered on Goatfell, the highest peak on the Isle of Arran, in July 1889. Imprisoned in Peterhead, he showed an exemplary character, was given a key role in the choir and found himself working as a prison carpenter. On 24 July 1893, he made his bid for freedom.

Laurie was working alongside other convicts on additions to the warders' houses outside the prison walls, under the eyes of a civil guard. It was early in the morning and there was a dense sea fog. Laurie grabbed the opportunity and leapt a fence, heading for the public highway. By the time the guards had spotted him and prepared to fire, he was vanishing into the fog. The alarm was raised, and it was a warder on a bicycle who first caught up with the fugitive on the road. As they struggled, other warders arrived to overpower him. When Laurie's prison sentence was completed, in 1909, he was moved to Perth Criminal Asylum, was regarded as 'of unsound mind'. There he remained until his death in 1930, though he was allowed the freedom of the town during the day.

The imagery of chain gangs in the United States is engrained within the popular consciousness. Escapes from the gangs were probably commonplace, but the risk of being shot or pursued by dogs, and thus killed or injured, makes such a brazen attempt into an act of pure bravery rather than strategy. But when **Robert Elliott Burns** escaped, it was with the specific purpose of standing up for his civil rights. It is partly due to his fight that Georgia's severe chain-gang system was eventually abolished.

Burns was a veteran of World War One, where he served as a medic. On his return to the States he found work hard to come by, eventually drifting into small-time robbery with some accomplices. He was given six-to-ten-years' hard labour for his part in a $5.80 grocery store robbery, in 1922.

Burns served on the chain gang in Campbell County (later called Fulton County), Georgia. One method of preventing escape was to feed the prisoners so little that they barely had any energy left after work, maintaining their focus on survival. Burns determined that Monday would be the best day to make a break for it, as his energy would have been conserved from the Sunday rest. He asked another inmate to sledgehammer his restraints, at the risk of seriously injuring his foot, in the hope it would distort them enough for him to wriggle out. As the guards dozed in the midday sun, his friend hit it three times. It contorted, and that evening he wriggled out of the chain on his ankle. In the middle of the night of 21 June 1922, Burns slipped out of the camp.

He made for a river and drifted downstream for a few miles,

knowing that the dogs would soon be in pursuit. His escape was greatly aided by meeting a hotel owner who had also suffered on a chain gang, and was therefore sympathetic to his plight. Burns made his way to Chicago where he worked hard at a new life, becoming the editor and publisher of *Greater Chicago Magazine*. He married, but, when he wished to separate seven years later, his wife turned him in to the authorities. His standing in the community was so high that people supported him in his legal battle.

Nevertheless, he agreed to go to Georgia to finish his sentence when the authorities agreed to let him serve a month or two of easy time. But when he returned their promise was not kept, and he found himself with at least twelve months of hard labour in Troup County. (If he had brought $500 to pay off the parole board, all would have been well.) After just over a year of imprisonment Burns escaped again, exploiting the trust he had built up with the guards who left him unchained as he worked. He managed to bribe a farmer to leave a car in the woods.

On his return to his hometown in New Jersey, Burns had difficulty finding work because of the Depression. But he was determined to do something about the injustice of his former situation and set about writing his autobiography, which was serialised in *True Detective Mysteries* magazine. It was a success. When he was rearrested in 1932, the Governor of New Jersey refused to extradite him since his book, *I Am a Fugitive from a Georgia Chain Gang*, and the film version – directed by Mervyn LeRoy, who had previously made the celebrated gangster movie *Little Caesar* – had turned public opinion against chain gangs.

The escape of **Frank Mitchell**, as 'masterminded' by the Kray twins, was something of a non-event. Put simply, Mitchell walked away from the working party on Dartmoor, met up with two of the Krays' boys from 'the Firm', and drove off to London a free man.

Frank 'the Mad Axeman' Mitchell was so-called because he threatened an elderly couple with an axe when he was on the run earlier. He had found the axe in a shed and forced them to watch television with him, whilst he drank tea with the chopper balanced on his knees. Or so the story goes. Another says that he was helping an old guy to chop wood when the police appeared and apprehended him. He had already escaped from two secure mental hospitals, Rampton and Broadmoor, and vowed to do likewise from any others he was committed to. As everyone noted, he was not insane but had the mind of a child.

In 1962 he was sent to Dartmoor. He settled immediately, and in a few years was off the escape list and allowed out to work in the quarry. Once he had served his time, he reckoned, he would be released. But in actual fact he had no fixed sentence, so it was up to the Home Office to determine his release date. By now his early days of violence in custody were over. He gave no one any trouble in Dartmoor and was liked by both the warders and the governor, all of whom knew how to handle him. Over six feet tall and very strong, he had gone from being a prisoner brutalised by the system to a trusty who wore a blue armband to indicate his status. The governor sought a release date for him, but the Home Office was not forthcoming.

In September 1966, Mitchell worked fixing fences outside the walls. These working parties on the moor often only had a single warder with them. Mitchell was regarded as such a safe bet that he freely left the work party and wandered away, spending time with the wild ponies that he tamed and rode, going for a drink in quiet country pubs and sometimes bringing back a bottle of Scotch for the night. For a while, he also had a relationship with a village schoolteacher. Another time he took a taxi to Plymouth, to buy a budgerigar that he kept in his cell. But no matter what Mitchell's day entailed, he would always be back by 4pm for collection by the prison van to return to his cell for the night.

In Wandsworth, ten years earlier, he had also befriended Ronnie Kray. Somewhere down the line, the Krays had given him their word that they would help him get out of prison, hopefully through their influence in high places. But as a potential member of the Firm, someone on the run and officially labelled a dangerous criminal was probably not the best idea. And a man of his size could not hide for long. The best bet was to urge the authorities to set him a release date.

Then the Krays changed their mind. Their other arrangements at the time were not going favourably. Ronnie's murder of George Cornell had backfired; everyone, friend or foe, was getting nervous. They needed some good PR. This, it seems, is why they decided to intervene.

For whatever reason, on Monday 12 December 1966, Frank walked away from the working party on Dartmoor for a rendezvous at midday with Teddy Smith and Albert Donoghue, at a phone box just off the road to Exeter in Horndon. It seems they were as surprised as anyone to see him casually walking towards them, hardly a furtive fugitive.

They had brought a change of clothing, including an old suit provided by Tommy 'the Bear' Brown, who was about the same size as Mitchell. They bundled all of his prison clothes together (along with his knife, explaining that it wouldn't be smart to get caught with it) and dropped it all behind a hedge.

Before the alarm could be raised, Mitchell was back in the London area, safely housed in a Barking flat owned by Lennie Dunn, who had a bookstall on Whitechapel Waste. The police had no idea where he was, and extensive searches of Dartmoor checked cars and combed the moors. The public were made to feel frightened.

The Krays' idea was to get the authorities to give Mitchell a release date. Teddy Smith penned his letter to send to *The Times*, directed at the Home Secretary, pointing out the injustice of being indefinitely incarcerated when he was not a murderer. Nothing resulted from it.

Mitchell was looked after at the flat by Donoghue, Smith and Billy Exley as his minders, along with 'Scotch' Jack Dickson and Dunn. They talked and played cards. But Mitchell was restless. He was not used to being cooped up in a small room for twenty-four hours a day. Now he couldn't even step outside the front door. And he wanted to see Ronnie Kray, but the twins kept putting it off. Reggie had problems of his own and tried to defer the issue. Ronnie was in hiding in Finchley, due to a complication whereby he was required to give evidence against a crooked police inspector.

Mitchell had a fearsome reputation if he became agitated. He was particularly strong, as his minders witnessed when he lifted a piano from the floor. They all thought he might turn up at the Krays' family home and cause a fracas.

The Krays hired a hostess from Winston's nightclub in the West End, Lisa Prescott, to calm his ardour. She got on well with Frank, who immediately fell in love with her.

In the meantime the PR plan for Mitchell's release wasn't working. The Krays had a man who was stir-crazy trapped in a basement flat. Mitchell had relieved Exley of his gun and was nursing it, feeling more secure with it in his possession. Reggie felt as if he was being threatened, and told what to do by Mitchell, in the messages that were sent out from the flat.

Ronnie got word to Freddie Foreman, to ask if Mitchell could be killed and disposed of. Foreman owed them a favour and, whilst not relishing the job, promised he would do it. (It wasn't until more than thirty years later that the full story appeared. As Foreman had already been tried for the crime and acquitted, at that point he felt he could freely divulge the details.)

In the belief that he was being taken to spend Christmas with Ronnie in the Kent countryside, Mitchell left his safe house on Christmas Eve at 8:30pm and was led to a waiting Ford Thames van in Ladysmith Avenue, with four men waiting in it. He was not pleased to be leaving Lisa behind, even if it was on the promise that she would follow. He must have sensed that something was wrong, for his murder took place more rapidly than anticipated. They had barely pulled away when Foreman and Alfie Gerrard set about him. Something in the region of sixteen bullets was unleashed before Mitchell was considered safely dead.

Mitchell's life of freedom had lasted for around two weeks. His body was never found. Perhaps he was buried at sea, his body taken by fishing trawler from Newhaven, weighted and dropped overboard. Others think he was cut up and cremated. As he was never caught, officially he is recorded as having made a successful escape from Dartmoor.

X
Taking Their Leave

John **Straffen** was a child murderer who escaped from Broadmoor. Within four hours he had killed again, strangling a five year-old whose body was found in a wood not ten miles away. Straffen's mental age was low. Some termed him as 'feebleminded', others as suffering from 'mental deficiency', both terms with specific legal definitions. At his original trial in 1951, the judge noted, "You might just as well try a babe in arms."

When Straffen was sent to Broadmoor, a hospital for the criminally insane, his intelligence was regarded as so low that it was deemed impossible to teach him a trade. But he was quiet and timid, not violent. He was only there six months before his escape, having discussed his intent with other inmates. The opportunity arose on 29 April 1952, when he was sent to clean some outbuildings on the Broadmoor estate. These buildings led to a small backyard bounded by the ten-foot outer wall of the institution. To aid his escape there were some large empty disinfectant cans standing around, which he used to climb onto the roof of the lean-to shed against the perimeter wall. He had only stepped out into the yard to shake his duster, his attendant later stated.

Over the wall, he ran towards the woods. It was 2:25pm. Four hours later, at 6:30pm, he was recaptured. During that time he had killed five-year-old Linda Bowyer. She had been strangled but not sexually interfered with. Straffen had planned the escape because he wore his own clothes under his work jeans, discarding them once free.

The locals had no way of knowing that anyone had escaped, as there was no public alarm signal. Straffen had knocked at one house and asked for a drink of water, then walked steadily towards Farley Hill, seven miles away, where he hung around. He was seen there, as was the child; both vanished at about the same time, just after 5:30pm. Fifteen minutes later Straffen appeared again, knocking at a door for a glass of water. He had come from the woods. He asked another woman for a lift to a bus stop, but asked her to halt and let him out when he saw uniformed men. Suspicious, the woman approached them when he had gone. They were male nurses from Broadmoor. Though he offered resistance, Straffen was easily caught.

The police went to Broadmoor the day after, once the missing girl was found, to ask Straffen what he had done during his liberty. He answered, "I did not kill her. I did not kill the little girl on the bicycle." Whereas before he had been regarded as unfit to plead, this time Straffen was made to stand trial. (It is highly unusual for the inmate of a criminal lunatic asylum to be tried as a sane man.) He remained locked up until he died in 2007, by which time he was Britain's longest serving prisoner, having spent fifty-five years inside.

Charles Bronson (the adopted name of Michael Gordon Peterson) wrote in one of many books penned within the walls of how he tried to cut his way out of Broadmoor, with an 'angel wire' (wire embedded with sharp diamond cutting edges). Though he worked through the night on the shutter, so that it was only hanging on by a thin piece of metal that he could snap, with a blanket held against it by his head to deaden the noise, he realised at 5am that he wouldn't be able to saw through the bar in the two and a half hours still left. So he postponed his escape until the following night, only to have his cell searched that day. Bronson, who was originally jailed in 1974 for robbery, has lived almost permanently inside prison since then, spending twenty-eight years in solitary confinement as a result of protests, hostage-taking and attacks on staff and inmates.

When **James Lang**, who had been sent to Broadmoor in the early 1970s for the rape and murder of a sixteen-year-old, escaped in 1981 and broke his ankle in the process, he knew that no one would shelter a sex killer. He limped off, but gave himself up a few hours later. When he was eventually released in 1985, he raped and murdered two women.

Alan Reeve also managed to get over Broadmoor's walls, in 1981. This time local people were alarmed. Straffen has not been forgotten. Reeve had been there since 1964, when he was fifteen years old, after murdering a friend. Around 1974, he began studying political theory. He obtained his Open University degree in 1980, and intended to continue with a PhD. However, though recommended for release since 1977, he was continually refused by the Home Office. And so Reeve decided he needed to release himself.

On 9 August 1981, using an improvised rope and a grappling hook made from a TV aerial, he escaped – though not without injury, as he went over two walls and a fence, and fell down twenty feet at one point. He broke bones in his back and foot, and tore his hands badly on the barbed wire. He was spotted by an inmate, but, unusually (particularly for a mental institution), his escape was not reported for an hour.

There was also someone waiting for him with a car, and he was spirited away before he could be recaptured. The car, hired by a young woman he had befriended three months earlier, would be found at Dover. The girl's parents lived in Spain, but Strasbourg was another feasible destination, as Reeve had discussed taking his case to the European Commission of Human Rights. In the event he went to Holland, where he and his partner believed they could find sympathetic political allies.

A year later, in Amsterdam, he became involved in an altercation over shoplifting a couple of bottles of spirits to celebrate his year of freedom, killing a policeman in the process. He was jailed for fifteen years. Inside, he studied for his doctorate in political psychology and later qualified as a lawyer. On his release in 1992, the Dutch judge refused to have Reeve extradited to Britain. For a while he worked in Holland, but later went to Ireland. When the British discovered he was in Cork, they asked for him to be returned to Broadmoor. Seventeen years after his escape, he returned – but only for five months, as he was now regarded as safe enough to integrate into society.

The 'Mad Parson' is how **John Edward Allen** was known after he walked out of Broadmoor in November 1947, wearing a parson's collar and stock front, a stage prop he regularly wore as a performer at concert parties for the inmates. His opinion of his own escape was that it was, "incredibly simple, and about as risky as walking carefully across Piccadilly during the rush hour." But he hadn't just walked out. It seems that he went over the wall, fell into some telephone wires that broke his fall and made for the main road. He wore his slippers initially, throwing them into a pond to put the tracker dogs off his scent. Dressed as a vicar, he was offered lifts to London, making his way to Paddington where he took the train to Devon. Allen had been sent to Broadmoor ten years earlier, in 1937, after strangling a seventeen-month-old girl, the daughter of a family he had befriended when he was working at a hotel as an assistant chef. It seems he was annoyed and frustrated at not having been chosen to bake cakes for a banquet. Allen was recaptured after two years, whilst working at a bakery in London. He was finally released in September 1951.

The escape of **Tom McCulloch** and **Robert Mone** from Carstairs Mental Hospital, near Glasgow, a comparable institution to Broadmoor, resulted in a night of horror that resembled some slasher-movie fantasy. But this was all too real.

McCulloch, who was in Carstairs after shooting a chef in the face for not putting enough butter on his roll, had met and struck up a homosexual relationship with Mone, who was serving life for the murder of a schoolteacher, committed when he was nineteen (followed by the rape of one of the fourteen-year-old girls in her class and the sexual abuse of another, neither of which he was tried for).

That night, in November 1976, was to set a new benchmark in Scottish criminal history. The two inmates were equipped with knives, axes, garrottes, fake ID, uniforms, fake beards, a torch ... and a rope ladder. They had managed to collect or make these weapons and tools themselves, hiding them in spaces between panels in the woodwork workshop, or in boxes. They had chosen a Tuesday evening because that was when the drama group met in the social club, away from the main wards. The drama group comprised McCulloch, Mone and one other patient. They were supervised by one male nurse, Neil MacLellan.

McCulloch and Mone were brought to the drama meeting, but not searched. McCulloch opened his box and strapped on a belt designed to hold knives and an axe. Both then went into the office where MacLellan was talking with the other patient. They pounced on both of them, throwing paint stripper in their faces, but the pair fought hard against their assailants. McCulloch had to chase the nurse into the corridor, wielding the axe to try to bring him down. When MacLellan disarmed him, McCulloch drew a knife instead.

Initially Mone was caught off-guard, not expecting this level of violence. But when McCulloch hit his accomplice for being feeble, Mone picked up the pitchfork and laid into the patient. Mone and McCulloch drew upon their arsenal, hacking both men to death with axes and cleavers. Mone finished the patient off by spearing him with a pitchfork, whilst McCulloch took an ear as a trophy.

They headed for the fifteen-foot security fence, for which they had prepared a rope ladder in order to get over the razor-wire. Once out, McCulloch, dressed as a male nurse, flagged down a car and explained there had been an accident. Fortunately, the driver's life was spared as a police car arrived on the scene at that moment. Instead, the two policemen bore the brunt of their brutally wielded axes and cleavers, leaving one dead, the other in a critical state. Meanwhile, the car driver went straight to Carstairs to try to explain that two of its nurses were engaged in a bloody pitched battle with policemen.

With the panda car as their means of transport, it wasn't long before icy conditions got the better of the two escapees and they crashed. Their next victims were a van driver and his passenger, who mistook McCulloch for a policeman and stopped to help – only to be savagely attacked and dumped in the back of the van.

Thinking they saw a roadblock, they detoured into a muddy field and got stuck. Raiding a nearby farm, they took a car and headed off southwards. They were finally apprehended when a police car rammed them on the A74 north of Carlisle. Both were given 'natural life' sentences and moved into the prison system.

In 2002 they sought to have their sentences overturned in the European Court, with the hope that one day they would be released. In 2007, the former schoolchildren from Dundee, where

Mone had committed his initial crimes, went public forty years after the event to relate their stories of that horrific day – including the girl raped in a classroom, who had never spoken about it in detail even to the police. They were intent on keeping these men from ever being released, whilst Mone and McCulloch had open prisons already in their sights, even changing their names in preparation for freedom. However, in a further twist, Mone had a fight in prison that could result in his release being rescinded. Perhaps the adverse publicity relating to his crimes triggered the clash, but the authorities have refrained from comment. Today he is back in the maximum-security jail at Peterhead.

To add to a hellish saga, Mone's father, a thief and a drunk, had decided he wanted to be more famous than his son. He made his bid by brutally murdering three women at a flat in Dundee. But his presence in Craiginches Prison in Aberdeen was not tolerated by the other inmates, and he was knifed to death in 1983.

XI
Room to Move

When one thinks of a prisoner escaping, one invariably has the image of a person in his cell searching for a way out. Classic images of the past predominantly consist of someone working away at a wall, or digging a tunnel to get out under the outside wall, or removing the bars from the window to squeeze through. Occasionally the door might be the way out, if one can get hold of a key, whilst attacking a guard necessitates the involvement of another. But our primary idea is of the person alone, battling against the insurmountable in order to achieve the goal of escape.

But nothing is quite so simple. Indeed, our ball is set rolling by **Johnny Ramensky**, who did not physically start his escape operation from the cell, but who epitomises the spirit of the escapee – to such a degree that the British government wanted him onboard for their efforts in World War Two, not only because he was useful with gelignite, but because he had the same spirit as those who worked for Special Services, even if his was channelled into criminal purposes.

Ramensky, a.k.a. 'the Gentle Johnny', for he never used violence, was famed as a safebreaker and escapee, having broken out five times in all from the bleak and isolated Peterhead Prison, near Aberdeen. His ability with explosives, which he learnt to use at fourteen when employed in the mines, made him an ideal candidate for war service. Whether he volunteered or was recruited, stories have been recorded of his formidable exploits with explosives. He is regarded as something of a hero on that front, though even as a criminal his reputation stands high, as he never robbed ordinary people, only businesses. It is said that, when he had money, he fed the poor (often without their knowledge), giving him a touch of Robin Hood. And whilst his escapes were always short-lived, they added to the reputation of a man who spent most of his adult life in prison.

To escape from Peterhead was perhaps more difficult than Dartmoor, because the conditions were more brutal, the landscape even bleaker. Ramensky's first escape, on 4 November 1934, is often put down to the fact that his first wife had died unexpectedly from a heart attack, and he had been refused permission to attend her funeral. (Other reports say she didn't die until 1937.)

In any case, he was in the prison hospital at the time. On that cold November morning, before anyone was awake, Ramensky picked the lock of the hospital block with a piece of wire. He escaped barefoot, creeping across the courtyard and scaling the outer wall, gaining toeholds in the mortar before hanging by his fingertips and dropping down. He set off on the hundred-and-seventy-mile trek to Glasgow, but was caught. The road south crossed two fast-flowing rivers, one at Ellon, the other at Bridge of Don. Roadblocks were always set up at both bridges whenever there was an escape and, though escapees might make it across the first in time, they never managed to arrive at Bridge of Don quick enough. Ramensky was caught in the back of a lorry at the first bridge, without any warm clothes, his feet bare and swollen.

He was taken to Craiginches Prison in Aberdeen to have his feet treated, before being returned to Peterhead, where he was shackled to the wall. Though the cuts turned septic, no medical attention was administered. Leather anklets were also fixed and the blacksmith welded rings of iron over them, to which chains were attached and joined to a leather belt around his waist. He was the last man ever to be shackled in a Scottish cell, wearing them for weeks without removal, even temporarily.

After he was released in 1938 he returned to safe blowing, which led to his speedy return to prison. In 1942, just prior to release, he was approached by British Intelligence and taken to the War Office in London, where he was asked if he would put his skills with explosives to use for the Special Services. They wanted him to parachute behind enemy lines to steal secret documents.

Ramensky's sentence was set aside, and he was sent for training at Achnacarry Castle in Inverness-shire to become a top-flight commando. Before he saw action, he served as an instructor, showing Allied Forces from America, France and Norway (as well as a contingent of former policemen) how to use explosives. It appears his achievements were many, though details of all the missions have never been made public. But it is known that he blew open countless safes in Germany, including at Goering's headquarters in the Schorfhleide. He also blew safes in Rommel's HQ, and in Rome he is said to have opened fourteen safes in one day when the Allies took the city. His discharge certificate read: "Military conduct exemplary. Honest, reliable man who possesses initiative and sense of responsibility."

Though his praises were sung from the top level, no sooner was he discharged in York than he heard there was a robber-proof safe in the city. Naturally, he proved the claim was false, and was caught and jailed for his pains. And so the cycle of his prison life restarted. Whilst inside this time, he thought to write his memoirs – which he did in secret, as it was forbidden at the time. He spent four years on the work. The day before his release, the manuscript was impounded and he was told it would be destroyed after three months. It was never seen again.

Ramensky had tried to escape again during that stretch from the hospital block, going over the wall and stealing a bike to get away. When he had escaped the previous time, albeit only for a few days, he had met a woman with whom he'd kept in touch. This time he was on his way to see her, but his efforts were thwarted – at the very same bridge, by the very same policeman.

On his release in 1955, he married the woman and was determined to go straight. And yet he was soon blowing a bank, his gains going either to the bookmakers or, more generously, to people living through hard times. He received ten years on capture. After a further three years' imprisonment, he knew he had to escape. Three such attempts are listed against his name in 1958: the first happened when he left the breakfast queue, forced a skylight and took a ladder to go over the wall; the next time he was found, tired and hungry, making his way across the fields.

His third attempt was more eventful, occurring during exercise period, which was held in the prison hall due to heavy rain outside. Ramensky slipped away and, using a copy of a master key, hid under the floorboards in the doctor's office. No one could find him. The policeman at the bridge believed he had finally found his way past. (It was said that the policeman's wife had already prepared a meal for Ramensky.) Instead, the escapee remained under the doctor's office, with an accomplice bringing him food.

After a few days, on Boxing Day, Ramensky came out from his cover and went over the wall. As the hue and cry had diminished, he made it as far as Persley Bridge at Aberdeen. At that point, the lorry driver who picked him up recognised him and called the police. Though he continued to commit crimes, and to be caught, he never escaped again and would die in prison. Towards the end, he had lost his touch with safes; one time he used too much gelignite and two passing policemen were blown off their feet, recalling that much-loved line from *The Italian Job*, when Michael Caine quips, "You're only supposed to blow the bloody doors off!"

We have already seen **Alfred Hinds** at work in the Law Courts. His ploy when escaping from prison on two other occasions was to ride on the backs of existing escape plans, and thus to avoid additional offences being lined up against him, all in order to boost his campaign to prove he was the victim of a miscarriage of justice. Both escapes are linked together because they are part of the same process. All emanate from this man masterminding both his own defence case and his escape plans from the nerve centre of his cell.

Hinds made his first escape from Nottingham Prison in cahoots with the robber **Patsy Fleming**. Hinds' agenda was to publicise his case against being fitted up over a jewellery robbery at the Maples department store in London. He was admittedly a small-time criminal, but he refused to take it lying down. After two years of incarceration, his appeal had been turned down, his petition to the Home Office dismissed. He only had recourse to one further option: to escape as a means of publicising his position.

Hinds' reasoning was that, in order not to leave himself open to a further charge for the escape, he would claim he was just responding to an opportunity: "I must not commit one crime in order to prove that I was innocent of another." If he didn't tell people he was planning an escape (which amounts to conspiracy), did not offer violence to a prison officer in the course of escaping, or perform any technical actions like making a key or drawing a bolt, then he was not, strictly speaking, responsible for the breakout. If another prisoner breached those same conditions, all Hinds could be accused of was 'escape from lawful custody' – which is not a criminal offence, just an offence against prison rules.

Patsy Fleming had reputedly planned a solo escape, but was happy for Hinds to help him achieve it. On 25 November 1955, during evening association when no one was looking, Fleming went through the grille door for which he had made a key, leading down to the stokehole. There he opened the flap on the coal chute and crawled up into a small well beneath a grating, for which he had to undo a padlock, before going out into the prison yard.

On the first night, the plan failed. Fleming came back covered in coal dust and had to be rushed to the washroom. The key for the padlock at the grating did not fit. The man responsible for making the soap impression had fluffed it, but would not admit to a bodged job. The next night, the escape method was repeated – though Fleming took along a hacksaw blade to get through the padlock, that process adding an extra ten minutes. Most importantly, eyes and ears had to be kept open to ensure that no one grassed, as the previous night's failure would have indicated an ongoing escape attempt to more than just the handful who were previously in the know.

This second night, Fleming went through the grating into the yard. He crossed to the workshop with intent to enter via the window, using a cramp to widen the bars. Then he discovered that the cramp was not strong enough. Instead, he climbed on the roof and broke through a wire-meshed fanlight to reach the two doorframes Hinds had made in the workshop, which could be fitted together to make a ladder. Unbolting the door, he propped them against the wall and went over. He had to rip a barbed-wire link fence from the ground, creating a gap to get through. Then there was only an eight-foot wall to climb over, aided by a plank of wood, before he paused for breath in the shrubbery of a private garden.

When Fleming had passed through the first grille, it was to be wedged with paper to stop it coming open. This happened, but only after Alfie Hinds had indicated he was following him down, once another inmate on lookout had seen from his cell that Fleming was in the yard, having broken through the grating. As Hinds saw it, he had followed in Fleming's footsteps.

The first Fleming knew of Hinds joining him in the escape was in the garden, when he heard a voice behind identifying himself. It was too late to argue. Fleming took Hinds along to meet the lorry that was picking him up. Hiding between orange boxes, they went through a roadblock and later transferred to a car, where they changed clothes and were driven to London. Hinds was provided with a mac and trilby to cover his prison uniform. Fleming would be caught three months later, on his home patch in the East End.

At least, that is the generally accepted story as taken from Hinds' published accounts.

He gives the credit for the escape to Fleming, making it appear that the other man was in control. But today, despite getting on in years and having never read Hinds' book, Fleming can still recall enough to make one understand how Hinds wrote the story to suit his own purposes. In fact the whole escape was planned and staged by him, with Fleming invited along. "I'd known him for ages," Fleming says. "I wouldn't have got away without him."

Details tumble out one after another, leaving us to fill in the other aspects. One cannot even be sure they tried to escape two nights in a row. But certainly, Hinds was down in the coal cellar alongside Fleming: "He stood on my head and killed me. He made the key for the padlock while he was there. We only had about ten minutes. Then he pulled me through."

There is no mention of a hacksaw blade, only of Hinds improvising his tools on the spot, using the basics he had brought with him. "The bell's gone and they were banging up and we haven't got out, we're still underneath. We're still working on that padlock."

Once Hinds had pulled Fleming through, and they had made their way across the yard to the carpenter's workshop, it was Hinds who produced the key for that door. "He could make any key."

They took out the frames they had made to get over the wall. Hinds went up and over first. "It was such a drop," Fleming recalls. Indeed, he had not realised how high it was until that moment. "When I got to the top, he'd gone down and … I would have broken my leg. He caught me as I went down. I would have knocked myself out coming down like that."

And so they made for the car that Hinds had arranged. "He had a motor waiting, a little bit away … Had a couple of suits that we put on right away as we were going along." As if to emphasise the respect and position Hinds commanded, Fleming adds, "The geezer who helped wouldn't have done it for me, but would have done it for Alf."

Hinds went his way to a cottage near Dublin, from whence he conducted his media campaign to have his case heard via his wife, Peg, at home in London. Out of necessity he started to study English law, using the National Library in Dublin. There he befriended a porter at Trinity College and started to attend criminal law lectures.

Then, after eight months, Hinds was arrested at gunpoint. He was aghast that the law was being flouted and that he was being taken back to England without the correct procedures – particularly as, in the way he described it, he had technically not committed the offence of escaping prison. His appearance at a magistrates' court, armed with law books, left the magistrate bemused, and he was sent to the assizes. Thus began the process of court appearances that led to the escape detailed earlier.

Hinds' next attempt at escape occurred at Chelmsford. As with Fleming, Hinds became part of the escape plan of **Georgie Walkington** – or at least that was how he wrote about it. On Sunday 1 June 1958, whilst many prisoners were at church, Walkington was supposedly cleaning his cell. He went down to the ground floor landing for a bucket of water, but his intention was to slip into a linen store and go to a hatchway, to gain entry to a passage to the bathhouse. In the linen store was an inmate who used it as a clubroom for himself and his friends to have a brew-up. Walkington persuaded him to let him go through to the double door at the end of the passageway, which he had a key for, and then out to the prison yard. He also had a key to the big gates that separated the yard from the compound.

It was more difficult for Hinds to slip his guard. As an escape risk he was not allowed to go anywhere without one, but sometimes they were slack. He asked to go down a level to get water but the guard was reluctant to go with him, asking Hinds to tell the warder below to shout up when he had arrived. Hinds had arranged for a friend to do the honours, whilst he went immediately to the linen store.

Hinds arrived as the storeman was bolting up behind Walkington. Hinds told him to open it as he was going too, catching up with Walkington as he was about to close the double doors. The two of them set off for the gates. The key didn't fit, so Hinds had the idea of taking two wheelbarrows used for carrying coal and pushing them to the wall, balancing one on top of the other and climbing up, hooking his denim jacket on the barbed wire to help haul them up. Hinds fell and broke his glasses, but eventually they both hauled each other to the top.

Once they were over the barbed wire, they worked their way

along the top before taking the twenty-five-foot drop to a path outside. Hinds hurt his leg in the process. Walkington went on ahead, whilst Hinds worked slowly through the graveyard until he reached the waiting Morris Minor. Walkington froze and said he had forgotten how to drive, so Hinds took the wheel despite his injured leg. Using only back lanes, he made for the Blackwall Tunnel and then on to Kent to stay with a friend of Walkington, who was not pleased to see the notorious Hinds until a substantial amount of money arrived to pay for his stay. Walkington was recaptured a little later, when he returned to his former haunts in London.

Hinds travelled back to Dublin the long way, driven by car to Liverpool, then taking the ferryboat to Belfast and the train to the Irish capital. Twenty months after his escape, Hinds was caught whilst smuggling cars from the Republic to Belfast. His hope that he would be charged and convicted only under his alias was dispelled, and he found himself back in Britain at the start of a new round of legal procedures.

His battle with the authorities showed them he was the equal of many a well-trained QC. The system tried to beat him down at every turn, until his old adversary, Detective Superintendent Sparks from the Flying Squad, published articles in the *Sunday Pictorial* in which he referred directly to Hinds. Hinds saw red and smelled a libel suit, a chance to argue in court that he had nothing to do with the Maples robbery. He won his case, and in the process was deemed innocent of his original conviction. He was ordered to be released by the Home Secretary, even though the Court of Appeal refused to quash the conviction. (When does the system ever admit defeat?) He went on to become a businessman, moved to Jersey, and joined the local branch of the high-IQ society, MENSA.

What is apparent from Hinds' case is the close understanding he had of legal matters. At least one judge during the years of legal process made comment on his abilities and the professional use he might otherwise have put them to.

George Blake did not make his escape from his locked cell at Wormwood Scrubs, as he was at liberty to move around the block up until the moment when he bade farewell. He was serving forty-two years for spying for the KGB whilst simultaneously working as an MI6 agent. Instead of being placed in a more secure prison, he was housed in the Scrubs, which was regarded as an easy place to escape from.

Blake did not give the impression that escape was even on his mind. He presented himself as an amenable person, teaching other inmates French and German, and teaching those who were illiterate to read and write. Perhaps he was kept at the Scrubs because it made it easier for MI5 and MI6 to interrogate him regularly. But, as Blake was not regarded as an escape risk, it seems that, once his interrogations were completed, he was kept there because it made it easier for his wife to visit!

If that was indeed the case, it seems remarkable. Blake was a spy who betrayed hundreds of British agents behind the Iron Curtain, perhaps causing a substantial number of deaths. It insults many other long-serving prisoners, and their wives and children, who have to trek up and down the country for years to visit their incarcerated men. It also says much about the British class system.

Blake's escape from prison occurred on 22 October 1966. He had befriended Seán Bourke, a murderer who was travelling back and forth from prison to a pre-release hostel. Bourke had acquired a walkie-talkie set and gave one to Blake, so that they could talk to each other once Bourke was ensconced outside in his bedsit.

Bourke had the assistance of two others who had promised to help Blake, anti-nuclear campaigners Michael Randle and Pat Pottle. Among other things, they gave Bourke money to buy a Humber Hawk car. On the evening of the 22nd, Blake had tea, watched wrestling on television and had a bath. At 6:15pm, wearing his plimsolls, he called Bourke, who was already sitting in the car outside the prison wall. It was a rainy, miserable evening. Blake went from his cell to the landing above, and climbed through a large gothic window at one end. Two of its panes and an iron strut had been broken and fixed lightly, to allow him to make a gap big enough to squeeze through. Then he dropped twenty-two feet to the ground, landing on a covered doorway halfway down to break his fall.

Bourke had to delay slightly, waiting for a courting couple to stop lingering and move on, before he could throw over a rope ladder with rungs made of size thirteen knitting needles. "At the twentieth rung, the one that would be nearest the top of the wall on the inside, I had wound two large knots of rope, one around each upright. These would keep the ladder a couple of inches out from the wall as it hung down and so make it easier for Blake to grip the rungs."

When Blake jumped down from the top he landed badly, cutting his head and breaking his wrist, though he didn't know it at the time. It only took three minutes for them to drive to rented rooms in nearby Highlever Road. It was a full ninety minutes after he had vacated his room around the corner before he was discovered missing.

Just before Christmas, Blake left for Germany in a Commer van, hidden in a secret compartment, with Michael Randle, one of the founder members of the Committee of 100 anti-nuclear action group, at the wheel. Randle believed that Blake's sentence was "unjust", and that "helping him was a decent human response". When they reached Berlin, Blake walked the final few yards through the checkpoint to the East. Bourke went to Moscow later to join Blake, hoping to start a new life. It wasn't for him, and he left for Ireland after two years.

When we talk about the great British escapees, we think back to that master of the art, Jack Sheppard, and his escapes from Newgate. His closest modern counterpart is **Walter Probyn**, whom I can only cover with a selective account of his *modus operandi*. His own book, *Angel Face*, gives more detailed accounts, as well as telling of a politicisation and immersion in law books which mirrored that of Alfred Hinds. As with some others in this book, both were intelligent men who, in their formative years, were socialised into less than constructive ways of living, as each would readily admit.

And so we also reach the practicalities of tunnelling one's way out of prison. For Probyn's crimes pale besides his many escapes. Set on a criminal path by unfortunate circumstances as a child, his response each time he was taken into custody was to escape, right from the very beginning. To detail all of them, even briefly, would take numerous pages, so we have to focus on the few that constitute his legend.

Probyn was called 'Angel Face' by the police and press alike, much to his annoyance, in an effort to convince the public not to be deceived by his "angelic countenance". He was ten when it all started, in 1941, incarcerated for stealing a discarded tin of peas. The violence and brutality shown towards him only made him resist all the more. At one remand home he stole a bunch of keys whilst still in the reception. Realising he couldn't use them, he handed them to the deputy headmaster and explained he had intended to escape. The deputy head handed him his empty cup and told him to take it to the staff kitchen, where Probyn discovered the window bars were wide enough and took off.

In his early days he was adept at escaping from police cells, often squeezing through the hatch in the cell door. He succeeded in five such escapes from Old Street police station. His method was to bang the hatch to make the catch jump, and to slide the hatch down at that precise moment. Once it was open, he could squeeze through and find the airshaft to climb up to the roof. Beryl Smith, his wife of ten years, whom he first met when they were still pre-teens, says he would also unscrew the grille of the heater in the police cell, climb in and pull it back in place. "Of course, when the law saw he was gone, they left the door open." His strength, she confirms, was that he always "took his time. He's got a lot of patience."

By fifteen he was already incarcerated in prison. He immediately set about digging through the floor of his cell at Wormwood Scrubs with a spoon, throwing the debris out of the window into the prison garden, or taking it out to the dustbin, concealing the hole with the black wax used to wax mailbag thread from the workshop. His aim was to reach the basement beneath, where he hoped to find implements to help him on his way. After piercing the inch-thick hard surface, the rubble beneath was easy. The skill was in trying to keep the surface hole small so that it did not collapse.

The hole became as deep as his arm, and he was ready to widen it. This never happened. He was moved to HMP Wakefield, where his attempts to saw through the bars were curtailed by prison grasses. His next stop was Rampton mental hospital in the north. Though he was not mentally deficient, as a doctor confirmed to him, he was a nuisance and an embarrassment to the penal authorities. At eighteen he was dubiously certified and incarcerated in the secure hospital. "I felt that among people who were mad, I would surely go mad before I got out."

Within weeks, in December 1949 he made an attempt to escape with another inmate, each shinning up separate drainpipes, climbing onto and racing across the roofs, just managing to jump a fifteen-foot gap at one point to a lower roof, until they made an outside wall at the far end. Resisting the temptation to go down quickly, they held out until they could escape into the fields. They were watched all the way, but only one guard was in a position to follow after them and he chose to pursue Walter's companion when they split up.

Prison Break

Probyn hid until nightfall in a ditch, before setting off across fields until he met the arterial road. By climbing to the top of a steep hill, he was able to jump onto a lorry when it was at its slowest and steal a lift to London. It was five months before he was recaptured.

In 1958 Probyn was in HMP Maidstone. "Maidstone is the only prison I've been to where prisoners regularly tried to escape and were chased round the prison by the screws but were not caught and remained unknown. It was the only prison I've been in that bears any resemblance to the comedy-film version of prisons." One prisoner he mentions "was cutting it a bit fine", sitting on top of the wall, joking and jeering about the holiday he was about to take, before disappearing. He reappeared not long after on crutches, still joking, but with both ankles broken.

Probyn got away from an outside working party at Maidstone in 1958, after his girlfriend had written that she was worried her children would be taken into care. In his efforts to move quickly, he took short cuts across allotments and climbed a fence, only to find himself in the local army camp amidst the officers' quarters. After he made his way down to the River Medway, he was determined this time not to get his clothes wet, as he had so many times during earlier escapes. Taking off his clothes, he fastened them with his belt to his head whilst he swam across, only for them to fall sideways at the last minute. As he noted, once you are wet you must keep moving to raise your body temperature and help dry out your clothes.

His capture this time came as the result of an act of stupidity. He was upset at the way the press made him out to be a dangerous gunman, and tried to arrange a meeting with a *Daily Mirror* reporter. It became a trap, and the police met him instead, followed by another front-page photo-splash and glorification of the event the following day.

Once in Wandsworth Prison, he swallowed carbolic soap in small balls to raise his temperature and feign the symptoms of appendicitis. He was taken to St James's Hospital in Balham, but was away through the hospital window, despite being barefoot and in pyjamas, after the nurse approached with a needle to knock him out for an emergency operation.

HMP Dartmoor had the characteristics of Alcatraz or Devil's Island, except that it was not surrounded by sea but by the moors. Though it was relatively easy to climb over the walls (the place was crumbling, footholds abounded and no rope or hook was really necessary, according to Probyn), or indeed to escape from working parties, everyone was afraid of the terrain and the climatic conditions of the moors themselves. If you kept to the roads, you were picked up. If you ventured off the roads you fell into a bog, or went around in circles, particularly in the pitch darkness of night.

Probyn had to depart anyway, because by this time he had married Beryl and heard, via others, that she was being pestered by an ex-boyfriend who had come out of prison. She tried to stop Walter from escaping, telling him to serve out his time, but nothing would shake him, she recalls. So they planned out the details together, but things moved quicker than intended:

"We went down to visit and Wally didn't know they were letting him out the same day, working outside. When we left the prison we didn't know until we got home that he had escaped."

Probyn had been sent out with a working party on 24 August 1964, to repair prison officers' homes at Princetown. He hoisted a bag of plaster onto his shoulder and walked down the street. Prisoners were not allowed to walk around in town unaccompanied, but who would show concern if a prisoner was lugging a bag of plaster?

It was foggy, which offered another advantage, for he had a compass with him that his wife had smuggled in on an earlier visit.

When he was out of the town he dropped the bag and set off towards the moors. The fog made good cover for moving around, but it also meant he came across other working parties quite suddenly and was almost caught. At one point, as Beryl recalls today, "he made a friend of a police dog and it was running along with him." Probyn always had a close affinity with animals.

Another time he went straight into a bog and had to carry on covered in mud. Though roadblocks were set up, visibility was short and, with no food or drink, he clung to his northeast trajectory, resting by day, walking by night. He made Porton after five days, where he was able to phone his wife's cousin.

"I found out on the news. But I'd already told him exactly what to do," recalls Beryl. "I said give yourself about four days to get away from the moor before you make any phone calls. I was up there with my cousin waiting on the phone call … He phoned and reversed the charge … I said to him, when you phone up your lorry's broke down. I shall say to you, 'Oh, you again, ain't it about time you got yourself a decent lorry? What you doing to these lorries?' I was having a go at him in case the operator was earwigging. And I says, 'Where are you this time?' He was in a little tiny village, God knows … Porton. That's where we picked him up. 'Stay where you are and we'll get to you as quick as possible.' And I also said to him, 'Whatever you do, don't steal nothing in the way of food or anything.'"

The car was already prepared with food, drink and clothes, so his rescuers set off immediately. They arrived in the early hours, parked the car, lifted the bonnet and made the agreed signs. Nothing happened. "The twat, he'd fell asleep. And all of a sudden I see this thing coming over the hedge. Frightened the life out of me. We stripped him naked and made a bundle of all his dirty old clothes, put clean clothes on him, give him a drop of brandy and sandwiches we'd took with us."

As they drove back they cleaned him further, doused him in deodorant as he smelt so bad, and fed him warm tea from a flask. Then they put him on the floor in the back, with Beryl and her cousin resting their feet on him.

This freedom lasted seven weeks. When he was taken back to Wormwood Scrubs he was badly beaten, receiving a broken arm that had to be operated on later as it was never set properly. Nevertheless, even in this condition he found a way to attempt an escape, but hadn't the strength to pull himself up the rope and over the wall with effectively only one arm.

His next trip was to the far north, to HMP Durham, where he immediately set about the cell windows – not cutting through the bars, but chiselling with a flattened and sharpened serving spoon handle at the cement around them. His new hobby became *papier mâché* modelling; besides making masks which he kept in his cell, it held his bars in place after a night's work. Though Probyn was physically fit enough for the escape, which required descending the wall with a rope, crossing barbed wire halfway down, then climbing a drainpipe and crossing more barbed wire, with the outer wall still to scale, his fellow escapee did not have the same strength and became stuck. Probyn climbed back up to release his rope, only to fall three floors and jar his spine badly.

When **John McVicar**, another robber, came to Durham's maximum-security E-Wing, he was determined to escape but wasn't sure whether he would find anyone serious enough to join him. Meanwhile, Probyn had discovered, when walking barefoot, that parts of the floor were warm and, when he stamped his feet, he could hear parts that were hollow. He knew that a hot water pipe system ran beneath his feet and, discovering a space behind a wall in the shower room, decided to investigate and see if it was a sealed-up chimney shaft.

Probyn brought in wire from the workshop concealed in his hamster cage, which he carted back and forth, pretending to mend its broken wheel. He also fixed chisels to weightlifting equipment, all of which went through the metal detectors without question. Whilst McVicar made a noise with the weights, Probyn chiselled away in the showers, filling his handiwork with *papier mâché* at the end of each session and covering it with emulsion paint. He was excavating through a small hole, removing bricks from the other side, a kind of keyhole surgery escape procedure. What fooled everyone, not only officers but inmates who knew an escape was in progress, was that no one could see it. Everyone searched the outer walls; no one thought that an inner wall would lead anywhere.

Debris was removed by wrapping small amounts in newspaper and pushing it around the bend in the toilets, to prevent blockage. Eventually, they worked down and broke into the ventilation shaft under their floor. When they made a hole that was big enough, Probyn went down to check out the lay of the land, using a rope to climb back up. He worked out that a bar had to be cut on a grille and a lock on the gate, and both then readied so that no one would know until they made their escape.

Probyn had done nine tenths of the digging work, whilst McVicar had been responsible for the lookout and the weightlifting distraction. They were almost caught when Probyn was making a rope in his cell as an officer walked in. "Effrontery is all one has in prison to rely on," so Probyn handed him one end, finished a stitch on the other and said thanks, asking the guard if it would be strong enough to hold a twenty-pound weight. The officer agreed, and left the cell.

Another time, Beryl made a surprise visit. "I nearly got him caught 'cos I went up there to visit without telling him. And the screws were running all over the wing looking for him … and he was digging underneath."

On 28 October 1968, Probyn and McVicar took their leave of their cells, taking **Joey Martin** with them. Martin had only come onto the wing the day before from Leicester, where he'd organised an escape plan. For both Probyn and McVicar, the joke of Martin escaping within a few hours of his arrival was irresistible. Charlie Richardson had earlier blackmailed his way into the escape plot as soon as he heard about it. Both Probyn and McVicar were adamant he was not coming with them because of his unpleasant demeanour and reluctance to contribute financially to a previous plan. They agreed to "blot him out" – though of course they omitted to tell him that. They were more concerned that Richardson would blow their escape in its final days than that the guards would discover them.

Martin went to look at books in the cell that served as a library and stood guard, whilst McVicar ran the rope out the library window and tied it. It would hang there unnoticed for two hours. Back in the shower room, they went through the hole, down the shaft and through to the cellar, finding their way to the grille and gate Probyn had prepared on the earlier test run. Once out, they used the rope they had planted to climb onto a plastic roof. It was a noisy affair, and unfortunately attracted the attention of inmates and staff alike – particularly Richardson, who was miffed to have been excluded and loudly yelled abuse.

With staff alerted to their overhead flight, it was not long before Martin was caught, though Probyn and McVicar managed to continue. On the roof of the courthouse they parted company. Probyn forced a trapdoor and went through the roof, into a court building, where he was cornered.

Outside the building, prison officers gathered. Two hours later, when staff gained entry, Probyn was sitting patiently in the waiting room. It was his last escape bid. From then on, he served his time up to release. Nothing was going to be made easy for him. In spite of the system's determination to prevent him from being anything but a recidivist, he started to read more widely, in sociology and law.

"It was the point where I changed my tactics of survival from escape to something more political." He wanted to lead a useful existence once he was free. In his autobiography, Probyn talks about arriving at Leyhill open prison and finding it a culture shock – as if they wanted him to walk out, so that they could lock him up all over again. He quietly refused, showing restraint and self-discipline, which the system probably claimed as its own success. Suddenly he was allowed out into the woods, alone, to clear the undergrowth, and to rediscover nature.

McVicar had continued across the roofs, eventually dropping down into the gardens of a row of terraced houses. Though he was chased by police, he made his way through the town until he reached the River Wear. "The sheer physical power of my running conquered my fears. This is what fitness is finally about – pulling it out when *everything* is at stake."

At one point, on waste ground, he fell and sprained his wrist. He also lost a shoe, and kicked off the other. He swam the river, and then later, after a rest in various yards and gardens, tried to leave the city by swimming downriver. It was bitterly cold, and he didn't make it too far. For three days and nights he kept moving, with the rain barely relenting. He was hungry and thirsty, but he managed to get out of Durham and make it to a small town, Chester-le-Street, where he was able to phone his girlfriend and arrange to be collected by two men.

McVicar remained free for almost two years. On 11 November 1970, he was recaptured in Blackheath at a flat above a dress shop.

"[I had] gained two years of freedom, during which I learned to love things I had forfeited before I even knew I wanted them." Since being released in 1978, he has worked as a journalist and commentator, after running through his life again in the book *McVicar by Himself* and its film adaptation, with himself portrayed by Roger Daltrey.

There had been an earlier escape by tunnelling from Durham in March 1961, when **Ronnie Heslop**, a soldier awaiting trial for stealing, dug his way out of his cell over a period of four days after removing a ventilation grille, using a teaspoon and kitchen knife as tools. His flight across the court roof led him to the river, which, like McVicar, he swam to get out of the city. He was recaptured six weeks later.

An escapee like Probyn can be likened to a hamster, or similar small mammal, finding its way out of a cage. This image also brings to mind Pentonville Prison during its rigorous Victorian regimes. Every morning the prisoners were taken to chapel, where each had their own separate pew. It was boxed much like an animal stall, with high walls so that inmates could not contact each other. Only the chaplain, perched on high, had an overview of the congregation bobbing up and down as they knelt to pray, or stood to sing. One time, a prisoner named **Hackett** did not pop up again. When the chaplain, looking across the sea of two hundred and fifty stalls, saw a gap, he sent the warder to open the box. It was empty. Hackett had lifted the floorboards and vanished. For some weeks he had been working at the boards, after studying the chapel from outside. He had noticed there was a gap in the outside wall for ventilation, which he suspected he could squeeze through if he could reach it from within.

Alongside Probyn, who had to face some of the greater problems of contemporary security, we have to place **Jack Sheppard**, the master of the art of escape in his day. Sheppard earned his fame as *the* escapee from Newgate Prison, which housed the holding cells for people awaiting execution at Tyburn. In a life that only stretched to twenty-three years, Sheppard was a notorious robber, burglar and thief, and an even more notorious escapologist.

His time and place was early eighteenth-century London. Sheppard won wide admiration not only for the audacity of his escapes, but also for the skill with which he accomplished them. His downfall was mainly due to one man, criminal-turned-thief-taker Jonathan Wild. Sheppard did not like Wild and, by choosing not to fence his spoils through Wild, set himself on a perilous course that ended at 'the Tyburn tree'.

Any thief-taker was anathema to Sheppard, who believed that they deserved the same fate (the gallows) as any thief, instead of financial rewards. Wild was also double-dealing as a receiver of stolen goods, which granted him control and power.

Sheppard's first prison escape was not his own; he was the architect of the escape of another, a simple but audacious affair. He had taken up a personal and working partnership with **Elizabeth Lyon**, known as Edgeworth Bess, a prostitute and skilled pickpocket whom he had met in a tavern, the Black Lion, off Drury Lane. Not long after, in 1723, she was caught and taken to St Giles's Round-house. When Sheppard went to visit her, he was refused entry by the beadle. His response was to knock the man down, break open the door and walk off with his mistress, Lyon, on his arm. Right from the off, Sheppard was gaining credentials among the criminal fraternity, particularly with 'women of abandoned character'.

Sheppard's own first confinement, in April 1724, and his subsequent escape attempt were also at St Giles's Roundhouse, where a magistrate had placed him for burglary. He was on the top floor. Sheppard gave his first effort a poor mark. "I had nothing but an old razor in my pocket, and was confin'd in the upper part of the place, being two stories from the ground; with my razor I cut out the stretcher of a chair, and began to make a breach in the roof, laying the feather-bed under it to prevent any noise by the falling of the rubbish on the floor."

Realising that a tile had fallen on a man passing in the street below, and that a crowd was gathering, Sheppard worked faster, ignoring the falling debris, lowering himself into the neighbouring churchyard with his blanket and climbing a wall. Though he was still clad in irons, Sheppard joined the crowd briefly. It was noted that he participated in their excitement, pointing up at the shadows and saying he could see the escapee. Then he departed. He had spent barely three hours within his cell.

The second confinement and subsequent escape occurred in New Prison, Clerkenwell. Lyon had also been locked in with him when she visited, suspected as his accomplice in pickpocketing a watch and believed to be his lawful wedded wife. They were housed in the Newgate Ward, the most secure cell. Or so it seemed.

But it was only a matter of days before they were out. Sheppard's friend and working companion, the robber Joseph Blake, passed him a file and other implements when he paid a visit. They filed through their manacles, with Sheppard's burdened by extra weights and double links, cut through a bar from the window and, using sheets and petticoats knotted together, lowered themselves to the ground. The makeshift rope was attached to the remaining secure bar, and Lyon went first – only to find they had landed in Clerkenwell Bridewell, the adjoining prison. Using gimlets and piercers as footholds, they climbed the twenty-two-foot enclosure at the gate to make their escape. This feat was quite extraordinary, as it should be noted that, whilst Sheppard was fairly small at five feet four inches, slight, nimble and deceptively strong, Lyon was a rather large and buxom woman.

The broken chains and bars were preserved by the jailers to commemorate the feat. Sheppard's earlier years as an apprentice to a carpenter had given him a good knowledge of the tools of the trade, as well as a great skill with locks. He still worked as a journeyman carpenter when he wasn't thieving (one might say when he wasn't in jail, but time actually spent there was negligible due to his escapes).

Sheppard's third period of confinement was thanks to Jonathan Wild, who plied Lyon with brandy in Temple Bar in order to discover his whereabouts. Sheppard had enjoyed three months of liberty, robbing coaches and breaking into shops. Wild could not allow him to continue to operate outside of his control, and so sought his arrest.

Sheppard was tried and found guilty of one of three charges of theft laid against him. He was sentenced to death. Imprisoned in the putrid smelling hellhole that was Newgate, he gained a stay of execution by the method he knew best: escape.

Newgate itself was as likely to kill you before you made it to the gallows. Walking past the place, one could easily be urinated upon from on high, or be the recipient of a chamber pot emptied from a window. Visiting times were rather liberal though, for the ratio of guards to prisoners was high, and thus sex, gambling, food or devices such as tools were more accessible than might be imagined. That said, during Sheppard's stay the pendulum was swinging towards a stricter regime.

When he was visited by Lyon and her friend, Poll Maggott, Sheppard loosened an iron bar in the hatch where visitors talked to the incarcerated. Whilst they distracted the guards, he slipped his slight frame through the gap in the grille. Dressed in women's clothes that his accomplices had brought with them, he was away.

Sheppard's freedom was short-lived. After an offence in Fleet Street, he was pursued by a posse, captured on Finchley Common and returned to Newgate – though not without an attempt to make a run for it, right at the entrance to Newgate itself.

Such was his fame that the queue to visit him was formidable. If they could pay the keeper, they could enter. Writers like Daniel Defoe came to speak with him; artists like James Thornhill came to draw him. But escape was not going to be quite so easy this time.

After a file was discovered, Sheppard was moved from the condemned hold to a strong room, the 'Stone Castle', "with my legs chain'd together, loaded with heavy irons, and stapled down to the floor." He thought it "not altogether impracticable to escape, if I could but be furnished with proper implements," but he was watched too closely.

One day, free of jailers, he looked around the floor and saw a small nail within reach, which he used to open the big horse padlock from the chain to the staple in the floor. Whilst alone, he would unfasten himself to stretch his legs. He was caught before he could resume his position one time, and thus felt obliged to show the jailers how he could open and close the padlock at will. They provided him with handcuffs to make it more difficult. He moaned and beseeched them not to bring such dread to him, whilst secretly knowing "that with my teeth only I could take them off at pleasure."

Within the hour he had released his cuffs and put them back on again. He even bloodied his wrists to gain compassion from the turnkeys, and any of the visitors or 'spectators' – which worked, as he was rewarded with quantities of silver and copper. Many of the visitors were wealthy and female, and would endure the stench to look at the prisoners. But what Sheppard wanted most was not money but a crowbar, a chisel, a file, and a saw or two.

His fourth escape occurred on the night of a disturbance next door in the court, after the enraged Joseph Blake had jumped his guards and slashed Jonathan Wild's throat with a small knife after Wild gave evidence against him. Wild was almost killed. He was certainly fortunate to survive, but, whilst he was recuperating and not paying attention to his trade, his world started to fall apart. This attack was the beginning of the end for him.

The distraction of the uproar gave Sheppard the signal to make his move, for he was under constant observation by his turnkeys until then. This was to be his greatest escape. On the next day, Thursday 15 October 1724, at 2pm, various officials visited and checked his restraints. After they had left, "just before three in the afternoon I went to work, taking off first my hand-cuffs; next with main strength I twisted a small iron link of the chain between my legs asunder; and the broken pieces prov'd extream useful to me in my designs; the fett-locks I drew up to the calves of my leggs, taking off before that my stockings, and with my garters made them firm to my body, to prevent them shackling."

He then made a hole in the chimney, up near the ceiling, and, using the broken links, wrenched out a transverse iron bar which effectively became his crowbar. He went up the chimney to the 'Red Room', which had not been used (or even opened) for seven years; there he worked on the lock's nut and soon had it off, opening the door. He also found a large nail to add to his collection of implements. But the door from the Red Room to the chapel was harder. "I was forc'd to break away the wall, and dislodge the bolt which was fasten'd on the other side." This created such a noise that Sheppard was surprised not to be discovered.

In the chapel Sheppard climbed over the iron spikes, breaking one off for his purposes, and opened the door on the inside by stripping the nut off the lock, as in the Red Room. In the 'leads', the rooms under the tiled roof, another door impeded his progress with its strong lock. All the time he was working in pitch black, "and it being full dark, my spirits began to fail me." But his spirits held, and, in less than half an hour, with the help of the nail and the spike, he wrenched the box off "and so made the door my humble servant."

A little further and another door blocked his passage, "being guarded with more bolts, bars and locks than any I had hitherto met with." He could hear the clock at St Sepulchre sounding 8pm. The box and its nut would not move, but he attacked the fillet of the door until the lock's box came off the main post. One further door into the lower leads, which was bolted on the inside, opened with ease. He clambered up to the higher leads and went over the wall. Then he realised that it was quite a drop – around sixty feet to the ground. Fearing that he might dislodge something and attract attention if he leapt to the adjoining property, he decided to return all the way back to his cell and retrieve the blanket. This he fixed into the wall with a chapel spike, before dropping onto the roof of a neighbouring house.

By now it was 9pm. The shops were still open, as was the garret door that opened onto the leads. He stole softly down two flights of stairs. His irons made a small clink, which was heard by people who thought it was a dog or cat. He then went back up to the garret and rested two hours, before going down again as the neighbour's visitors were leaving. Within the hour he became determined to go, first tripping and making a noise before he made a rush for the street door "which I was so unmannerly as not to shut after me."

Now free, he took a route through Holborn and Gray's Inn Lane into the fields; at 2am he came to Tottenham Court, taking refuge in an old barn where cows had been kept, to rest his swollen and bruised legs. He discovered he had between forty and fifty shillings in his pocket.

It rained all day Friday, but that evening he ventured out and found a little blind chandler's shop where he obtained some food and drink. He rested again through Saturday and Sunday, trying with a "stone to batter the basils of the fetters in order to beat them into a large oval, and then to slip my heels through." He was discovered by the master of the shed, but told the sob story of being an unfortunate man sent to Bridewell for fathering a bastard child, who had now made his escape. Though he drew sympathy, the man wanted him gone. Sheppard put his trust in another man he came across, offering him twenty shillings if he could get him a hammer. This man, a shoemaker, had a blacksmith for a neighbour and brought tools along. "That evening I had entirely got rid of those troublesome companions my fetters, which I gave to the fellow, besides his twenty shillings, if he thought for to make use of them."

Damaging his clothes to appear as a beggar, Sheppard had a square meal in Charing Cross, overhearing tales of his exploits from those gathered there. And so it was the next day; wherever he went to eat or drink, or mix with the crowds, all he heard was talk of his escape. He sent word to his mother, who visited him in a lodging he took and begged him to leave "the kingdom". But Sheppard was a true Londoner and had to remain close.

He broke into the Rawlins brothers' pawnbroker shop in Drury Lane. Though he disturbed the occupants in the next room, where they slept, he talked as if he was not alone, "loudly giving our directions for shooting the first person through the head that presum'd to stir". Thus he left with his booty, appearing the next day "transform'd into a perfect gentleman", and then ventured with his new 'sweetheart', Kate Keys, back towards Newgate to a public house, to become "very merry together". After driving past Newgate Prison itself in a hackney coach, that evening they all drank brandy with Sheppard's mother in Sheers' alehouse in Maypole Alley, near Clare Market.

In his own words (the rest of the account quoted here was probably ghost-written for him by Daniel Defoe – author of *Robinson Crusoe*, and more especially *Moll Flanders*, which uses Newgate as a location), signed just prior to his death on 16 November 1724, he continued, "and after leaving her I drank in one place or other about the neighbourhood all the evening, till the evil hour of twelve, having been seen and known by many of my acquaintance; all of them cautioning of me, and wondering at my presumption to appear in that manner. At length my senses were quite overcome with the quantities and variety of liquors I had all the day been drinking of, which pav'd the way for my fate to meet me; and when apprehended, I do protest, I was altogether incapable of resisting, and scarce knew what they were doing to me."

Some attributed his great feats to assistance from the Devil. But his skill lay in his use of tools and his dexterity. This time he was placed in the Middle Stone Room so that he could be watched at all times, and was also burdened with three hundred pounds of iron weights.

Naturally he intended one final escape, en route to Tyburn's gallows. He had a penknife in his pocket, with which he intended to cut the cords binding him, and then to throw himself from the cart into the crowd, making his bid through the passages around Little Turnstile, where he knew the narrowness would prevent the horses following, and where he expected some assistance to be offered by the crowd.

But this was not to be. The knife was discovered just prior to his departure from Newgate. Of course, Sheppard could have avoided the gallows, but the price was to inform on his associates. Though he had been the victim of others who betrayed him, he scoffed at any such idea, preferring to face the death sentence. This was only to be expected. A villain he undoubtedly was, but his individualistic stand against authority and skill at escaping – and indeed his sense of humour, when one reads his written accounts – merit him an afterlife of fame.

Sheppard has been the subject of songs, poems and even plays, some as soon as he was taken down from the gallows. He was also the model for Macheath in John Gay's *The Beggar's Opera*; Charles Dickens used him as the basis for the Artful Dodger, and William Hogarth as the inspiration for the Idle Apprentice in his series of engravings, *Industry and Idleness*. At one point, it was feared that his popularity was gaining so much ground that others would emulate his behaviour. Consequently, all licences for performances were refused for plays that contained his name in the title. This fame extended beyond England. In the Wild West, Jesse James and his brother Frank signed letters to the *Kansas City Star* as Jack Sheppard.

Whilst Sheppard, the most famous jail escapee of all time, had made a mockery of Newgate Prison's security, others were willing to travel to the lower depths where he had clambered upwards. In 1731, six prisoners who broke through a dungeon floor braved the nauseating filth of the sewer beneath. Two were drowned and their skeletons found later, but the others escaped. The robber **Daniel Malden** escaped the condemned cell in 1737 and made his way to freedom through a sewer. He fled to Europe, but returned, was recaptured and hanged.

Newgate was one of the main targets of the mob during the Gordon Riots. They first demanded the release of the prisoners. The keeper refused, then had to flee over the roof with his wife and daughter as the mob stormed the building. All the furniture, together with doors, floorboards and a collection of pictures, were piled up against one of the walls and set alight. The mob then freed all three hundred prisoners, including four footpads who were to be executed the next day. The building was burned out and had to be rebuilt.

It seems that there was an American Jack Sheppard, who worked from the 1850s onwards around New York. Though one can read of his early exploits with Italian Dave, a kind of Fagin figure, once **Jack Mahaney** graduated from his apprenticeship, and became his own boss, he worked under aliases that make him difficult to track. However, it is known that he was an expert escape artist, twice escaping from Sing Sing and twice from the Tombs prison in New York City, as well as others. But details of these escapes are sketchy.

Jean-Henri Latude sent the Marquise de Pompadour a box of poison in 1749 and informed her of a plot against her life, apparently all for a joke. His sense of humour proved disastrous. It was not appreciated by the French King's mistress, and he was cast into the Bastille for fear that he was part of a political conspiracy against the monarchy. Despite three escapes, Latude spent thirty-five years of his life in prison.

His first escape was from the castle keep of Vincennes in June 1750, after being transferred there from the Bastille. He was closely watched, but had lulled the guards by always walking ahead and down the steps to the garden quickly for his recreation. They knew he would always be waiting at the bottom – until one day when he wasn't. He had scurried down fast and walked straight out, encountering an open door in the garden, slipping past its guard and away into the fields. All his gaolers and guards that day were locked up in the Bastille for a few months, until it was ascertained they had not participated in his escape.

Later that day, Latude went back to Paris in search of his old friends. There he came across Annette Benoît, whom he had met just before his arrest. She tried to help, but his older friends were mindful of punishment if caught. He was recaptured within five days, as was Benoît. She only received a two-week imprisonment when she pleaded 'love' as mitigating circumstances.

Once back in the Bastille, Latude shared a cell with **Antoine Allègre**, who was incarcerated for a similar hoax involving the Marquise. Determining that escape was the only solution, they found that a chimney was the best route out, even if it was spiked with gratings and bars and the eighty-two-foot drop to a large moat was daunting. By lifting a tile, they discovered that beneath their cell was a space between the floor and the ceiling, enough to store any tools or objects needed for their escape. They set to work removing the blocking bars in the thirty-foot chimney, and making a rope ladder of around eighty feet to get down from the towers.

It took them eighteen months of working at night. They unravelled shirts, handkerchiefs, towels, stockings, breeches, anything they could to twist the threads and extend their rope. Their consumption of materials was enormous, but they managed to secure extra clothing. Inside the chimney, it took six months to clear the barriers. The ladder they constructed had a hundred and fifty-one rungs, each made from sawn fire-logs covered in cloth to avoid making any noise against the wall.

On 25 February 1756, Latude and Allègre started to prepare for their escape as soon as their dinner was brought to them at 6pm. By 8pm all was prepared at the foot of the chimney: ladders, ropes, tools, even some brandy. Latude set off first, and then everything was hoisted up the chimney. When they came out of the top, they climbed down onto the platform and took the rope ladder across to the Trésor Tower, where they fixed the ladder to a cannon and lowered it to the moat. With a safety rope attached to Allègre, Latude went down first. After all the rest of the equipment, plus a portmanteau with some clothes, was sent down, Allègre joined him. They were determined to go through the moat wall. Standing in freezing water up to their chests, they worked at removing blocks. Even after piling aside several dozen, they felt they were getting nowhere. It was almost dawn before they breached the wall, and then changed into the clothes they had brought in the portmanteau. Latude wasn't recaptured until June.

When Latude was finally sent back to Vincennes he was watched closely, with an extra guard added for his daily walk in the garden. One day in November 1765, there was a fog hanging over the garden. Latude turned to a guard and asked what he thought of the weather. The guard said it was bad. Latude retorted, "I myself find it very good for escaping." And, before the guard could react, Latude was off and running. Within seconds he was lost in the fog, other guards only spotting him briefly as he sped past. At one point, with everyone screaming, "Stop! Stop!", Latude joined in, shouting and pointing into the distance. When he arrived at the front gate, the guard was ready with his bayonet fixed. Latude slowed and quietly approached the man, whom he knew. "Your orders are to stop me, not to kill me." Before the guard realised that Latude was too close, the prisoner had overpowered him and pushed him aside, before taking off into the fog. This escape lasted for three weeks.

In 1775 he was moved to Charenton, the madhouse, and let out a couple of years later on the proviso that he retired to his hometown. Needless to say, he didn't obey and was imprisoned again. It was only by the chance intersession of Mme Legros, who had read of his plight, that he was given a definite release in 1784. What started off for Latude as a youthful prank ended with him a broken old man emerging from prison.

Our focus in this book has been mostly on modern times. But a few words can be added about the kings, queens, nobles and conspirators who traditionally made their escapes from fortresses and castles. These strongholds have always housed prisoners, and thus escapees. If we take the Tower of London as an example, we see that it housed prisoners of high rank along with religious dissidents. For eight hundred and fifty years it served mainly to house political prisoners. Only a few ever escaped its high walls and deep moat.

In fact, the Tower's first prisoner was also its first escapee. **Ranulf Flambard**, the Bishop of Durham, was imprisoned in August 1100 for extortion in his role as tax collector. In February 1101, his friends smuggled in a rope in a wine casket. Having entertained his guards with the wine, as they slept happily he tied the rope to the window of his cell in the White Tower and climbed down, dropping the last twenty feet when the rope ran out. A ship had been arranged to carry the bishop and some of his treasure, along with his elderly mother, to a refuge in Normandy.

In 1244, the Welsh prince **Gruffydd ap Llywelyn Fawr** tried to escape from the White Tower after King Henry III reneged on a deal and held him hostage. Impatient for diplomacy to free him, he tried to escape from the top floor of the tower using a rope improvised from bed sheets and cloths. But it broke under his heavy weight, and he was discovered the next day by the yeomen, having fallen ninety feet to his death.

In 1597, **John Gerard**, a Jesuit priest and writer, escaped with **John Arden**, a fellow priest and fellow prisoner, from the Salt Tower where he was held as a practicing priest during the reign of Queen Elizabeth I – a time when Catholics were persecuted and priests found guilty of treason. Gerard hacked at the stones around the door to his cell, sneaked past the guards and met up with Arden as arranged. They found their way onto the high wall overlooking the moat. Below, waiting for them, were supporters who threw a rope attached to a small iron ball. Tying it to a cannon, they inched down to the moat and into the waiting boat.

Politics played its part in **Ian Fraser** making his escape from Al-Ould Prison in Riyadh, Saudi Arabia, in December 1980. Fraser had been caught up in the repercussions of a diplomatic dispute after a British television film, *The Death of a Princess*, depicted the Saudi justice system as barbaric, resulting in a crackdown by the authorities on British workers in the country. Fraser was one of those jailed for violating the country's alcohol laws. His long jail sentence made him a political prisoner in the Saudis' tussle with the British government.

The high-security prison seemed possible to escape from, even though it had never been done before. Fraser found a partner, **Eric Price,** and in the dead of night they went from their cells to the bathhouse, working loose the bars on a window. Once in the yard, they tried to break the padlock to a gate. It took them forty-five minutes, during which time the guards had stayed indoors in the watchtower because it was raining. Nevertheless, the area was still brightly floodlit, and they were lucky not to be seen. Outside the prison they had arranged for a car to be left along the road, paid for by relatives back home, containing keys and fresh identity papers. They drove fast because they expected early discovery, as Muslims in the prison awoke before 4am for prayers. There were no problems at any of the barrier points on the roads as the guards were asleep. Arriving at the coast, they obtained a boat and sailed for Bahrain, making three efforts to land before they successfully found themselves outside Saudi territory. In the event, when they were discovered missing they were assumed to have gone in the opposite direction, to Jeddah. All efforts to catch them were focused on the road that led across the desert.

The image of a prisoner scooping dirt with a makeshift trowel from the floor of his cell is hard to dislodge. Instead of going over the wall, some escapees have found it possible to go under. There is more potential for this approach in prisons built on sand beds or other manageable soil. In August 2003, eighty-four Brazilian prisoners made the largest escape in their country's history at the top-security

Silvio Porto Prison, in the state of Paraiba, by excavating a tunnel that was one metre wide and ran for fifty metres. It was even lined with lighting. The total could have been higher, but forty-one had declined the offer to join the escapees. After the fact, the prison admitted that the inmates had seemed a little restless in recent times, but that guards had refrained from searching their cells, either out of fear for their own safety or because many of those working in the prison were in the pay of criminal networks.

Long Kesh (later known as the Maze), outside Belfast, had a history of tunnelling because it stood on sandy soil. It has been estimated that over two hundred tunnels existed beneath the prison, and it wasn't unusual for those trying to escape to come across other abandoned tunnels. Not all went towards the perimeters and some have been found that burrowed backwards, further into the heart of the camp. Few tunnels seemed to be actually finished. In November 1974, thirty-three IRA prisoners made their way along a sixty-five yard tunnel that came out just beyond the perimeter wire. Most were recaptured immediately, whilst Hugh Coney was shot dead by a sentry. The three who escaped were captured within the day.

Before the 'Great Escape' of 1983, the most successful mass escape from Long Kesh took place in 1976, when twelve IRA men went down a trapdoor in a compound hut and along a forty-foot tunnel, negotiating five old tunnels and seams of concrete that had been poured into them. They were expecting to surface outside the boundaries but found themselves faced with a high wire fence and, beyond that, an army watchtower, floodlights and a twenty-foot wall. The tunnel was too short. Remarkably, they were equipped to deal with such obstacles, going through the fence with bolt cutters and climbing the wall with the aid of a grappling hook. Nine got away. Let down by their backup people, they had to walk to the motorway. It was not until two were picked up by the Royal Ulster

Constabulary, eight miles from the prison, that the authorities found out anyone had escaped.

Willie Sutton, also known as 'the Actor' for his disguises, was a bank robber who was looked upon kindly by the people – not because he was a Robin Hood character, like most others he kept the money for himself, his high living and immaculate dress sense. But Sutton was not violent. Indeed, he was seen as overly polite, like an usher at the cinema, as someone noted – though he did point the way with a gun rather than a torch, even if he never fired it in all his years of robbery.

He also found fame as a habitual escapee. Sutton was proud of his escape from Philadelphia County Prison in Homesburg, Pennsylvania, for it followed the same application of his law of the obvious as his robberies. The idea had come "when I saw an armoured truck stop in front of a business establishment after closing hours. Two of the uniformed guards approached the door, rang the bell, and were admitted. In a few moments they marched from the store, climbed into their truck and drove off … I doubted very much if the clerk who admitted them to the store looked at their faces. He saw the uniforms and waved them in. The right uniform was an open sesame … that would unlock any door."

So why not apply that principle to an escape? If inmates were walking across the yard at night, carrying a ladder and dressed in prison officers' uniforms, they might not be challenged. "I had to make them think I had a right to be out there doing something with a ladder." And what better time to do it than when the weather changed? Winter was upon them. Sutton waited for a snowstorm, as it might entail sudden emergency repairs. That is exactly what happened on 10 February 1947. When the prison searchlight pinned him and his four accomplices down, Sutton waved and said it was okay. They were left to proceed with their escape.

Prison Break

Sutton – who spent a lot of time in prison reading philosophy, economics, geography and political science, claiming, "I would never allow them to imprison my mind" – made a relevant comment: "Planning to escape from prison takes infinite patience. Precision work spaced over a long period of time. A plan which can be described in a paragraph may have taken two years to put together."

3 April 1945 is a classic example, when he and others tunnelled out of Eastern State Penitentiary in Philadelphia. Though Sutton is credited with the escape plan, it was a plaster worker, **Clarence Klinedinst,** and his cellmate, **William Russell**, who planned it and dug into the wall of Cell 68 in Block Seven. They went fifteen feet down, and ninety-seven feet out to Fairmount Avenue, then a further fifteen feet up to the street. The tunnel was shored with wood and equipped with lights. On the way to breakfast that morning ten inmates joined the escape, including Sutton, emerging near the corner of 22nd Street and Fairmount. Sutton's freedom was short-lived, a matter of mere minutes. All the others were recaptured too, some quickly. One even rang the prison doorbell early one morning a week later and asked to be let in, as he was famished. Klinedinst, who had just a few months left before his parole, was given twenty-five years for the escape bid.

This way of escape is largely a thing of the past in Britain. The materials from which today's prisons are made are more formidable, and to excavate the ground itself is possible in only a limited number of places, as noted. **Roy Webb,** known as 'Rubberbones', escaped from Dartmoor Prison in November 1951 by tunnelling out. He started in his cell, digging nightly with a needle, washing away the concrete debris each morning when he slopped out. He did not have to tunnel the whole way, for he came across an old disused tunnel that came out close to the wall.

In those days there were not regular security patrols like today, thus getting a rope and hooking it over the wall was more feasible. And yet, like so many escapes, unless it was organised on the outside then the escapee could fall foul of the most unexpected glitch. In Webb's case, once he was back in London he was reported to the police by a barrow boy to whom he tried to sell clothes. But Webb was a regular escapee. At Wandsworth Prison at the beginning of the 1960s, the staff baited him by suggesting that Dartmoor was too easy to escape from, unlike their prison. Webb proved them wrong, even if his freedom only lasted a few days.

As has been noted, some prisoners have escaped through the roof. But using a can opener is not something that happens every day. **Ralph Phillips** did just that, cutting his way through the corrugated metal roof of the kitchen unit in the Erie County Correctional Facility, Alden, New York, in April 2006. Attention was focused not so much on the escape as on the crimes he committed on the run, and the subsequent shooting of a state trooper on a stakeout, waiting for him to show at the home of a former girlfriend. For a while it was not believed that Phillips had committed the murder, as he had a history of non-violence, his crimes being mainly burglary. He was caught the following September.

Timothy Vail and **Timothy Morgan,** one a rapist and murderer, the other a career criminal jailed for murder, made their way from Elmira State Penitentiary, New York, in early July 2003, by gouging their way through a five-inch thick, steel-reinforced, concrete ceiling in their cell.

Once they had squeezed through the ceiling, using plastic bags to line the opening and protect themselves, they crawled across the electric wires and plumbing until they reached the ventilation shaft. After removing the covering they rubbed themselves with Vaseline and baby oil to ease their bodies through the shaft. It was fifteen feet long. Once they emerged through the screen they jumped five feet down onto the roof and then used knotted sheets to lower themselves down a sixty-foot outer wall, the end tied to a short ladder between two roof levels.

Vail, however, got tangled in the sheets and fell the last thirty feet, fractured his collarbone and tore ligaments in his leg. He was unconscious for two hours. Morgan stayed put, undecided whether to climb down or not, expecting the guards to arrive at any time. Eventually, when Vail regained consciousness Morgan went down to him. The headlights of a truck pulling into the parking lot froze them both, yet the driver, a prison officer, had not seen them. Again they didn't move, expecting guards to appear at any moment. When the driver returned, he drove away without even noticing the dangling bed-sheet rope. They departed for the woods.

A chart discovered later showed they had started to work towards their escape in early March, just after they moved into a new cell at the top of their four-storey block. They had stolen a broken sledgehammer, a four-inch drywall screw, blades and other bits from the prison workshop. Rather than paint their walls, or pin up glamour images, they painted their ceiling black. Whilst lying on the top bunk, Vail chipped away at the ceiling in the corner near the bars, flushing the pieces down the toilet. Guards rarely entered the cells, and from outside they could not see the hole that was developing.

When they acquired the hammer by good fortune after a civilian supervisor had to leave early, Vail returned to his cell from the workshop early too, thus missing the metal detector scanning procedure. After that they worked more quickly, the noise of the television drowning out the sound of their work. Each night they covered it with painted cardboard held in position by chewing gum. Eventually, when the hole was big enough, Vail looked through and found it led to the roof space. The maximum hole-size they could risk was eight by eleven inches, so they dieted to be able to squeeze through.

Once into the space, they found a ventilation shaft that led onto the roof. The props needed for their escape were stored up there. Plastic bags filled with rags and paper were left as dummies in their bunks, their own hair clipped and stuck on at the last moment to round off the faces they had painted. They also collected bed sheets, holding back some of the soiled ones and buying others from mail-order catalogues, knotting them together and securing them every six inches with masking tape until they had a sixty-foot rope.

The alarm was not raised until 6:30am, six hours after they had left, when a guard entered to wake them after they did not respond to his orders. Though they holed up in an abandoned trailer camper whilst they took stock of Vail's injuries, they vowed to press on, taking beer, food and clothes from a nearby house. Like many escapees, their plans extended as far as getting out of the prison, not to what they would do once outside its boundaries. Given Vail's injuries, they took greater chances than they might otherwise have done, at one point stealing a Dodge van that still had its engine running. It was only a matter of time before they were apprehended.

The last escape at their maximum-security prison had been almost twenty years before, in 1984. Built as a juvenile-detention facility, it had no perimeter fencing. The administration had been intending to address some of the security issues for the previous twenty years, but budget cuts took precedence. The result was that there were no guards in the towers at night, no sweeping searchlights, no razor-wire, no cameras …

The fame of **Giacomo Casanova** lies in his seduction of women, the life of love which he wrote about. In 1755 he was arrested and denounced as a 'magician'. He was imprisoned in the space under the roof of the Doge's Palace, 'the Leads', as it was known because of the thick lead plates on the roof, which became unbearably hot at times. It was not easy to escape. He had been initially placed in another room, from which he was trying to dig out, but he was moved before completion of his plans – though he did manage to salvage the iron bar spike and transfer it with him.

In another cell was a monk, **Father Balbi**. Knowing he was to be closely watched, Casanova smuggled the spike to the monk, hiding it in a folio edition of the Bible that he sent round with a big dish of *gnocchi* as a present to celebrate St Michael's Day, bringing Balbi in on the escape plan. The priest broke through a hole in his cell, and came down a corridor to break a hole into Casanova's ceiling, so that he could climb through. They pried their way through the lead plates onto the sloping roof of the palace, but, finding the drop to the canal too great, they managed to pry open a dormer window. Moving a ladder they found on the roof, they lowered themselves into an office of the palace, making their escape in the morning, once they had rested, by moving through some galleries and chambers until they found an outside door. When it was unlocked by an official, they pushed past the man and rushed away to find a gondolier. Casanova left for Paris, where his escape granted him celebrity in 'good society'. All this is described in a couple of paragraphs, but Casanova's extraordinary memoirs are in great detail, with every move well-documented.

Gerard Tuite, the IRA bomber, started work on escaping the moment he arrived at Brixton Prison in December 1979. Boring into the cell wall, he halted when he struck the steel mesh and granite beneath the plaster. Later, when he was moved to the maximum-security D-Wing, it was to a cell on the bottom landing. He thought his best way out was through an end cell on the first floor, and manipulated matters to make a switch with its occupant.

The cell next to him was occupied by **Stan Thompson**, who was on remand awaiting trial for armed robbery, and next to him **James Moody**, a notorious robber. But as far as the authorities were concerned, Tuite was the main catch and had to be watched.

Thompson already had a notable escape from Dartmoor under his belt some years before, breaking through the cell window, climbing the wall and fleeing onto the moor with two others. "To some of us, escaping is the only way we can keep our sanity. We gotta know there's a chance to get out otherwise we might as well give up on life." Although Thompson had studied the Ordnance Survey map, they still came a cropper and were recaptured.

Tuite thought that if he went through his cell wall, he would get out onto a roof. Moody and Tuite resolved to work together, as Moody also had plans to vacate the premises. He had tungsten masonry bits, screwdriver bits, hacksaw blades and superglue tubes brought into prison via his brother and family, hidden in socks as the scanners did not go that far down the visitors' legs.

Initially the men improvised a drill from a discarded pencil sharpener, but it was too slow. Moody suddenly developed a passion for large jigsaws that required him to bring a sizeable table into his cell, one that conveniently had a tubular bar ideal for the hole-boring process.

The first hole in the wall, made between Tuite's and Thompson's cells, was concealed behind a cupboard in Thompson's room. Then Tuite set about his outside wall, covering it with cardboard, placing paintings and a cabinet in front of it. Moody's was the last to be done, linking him through to Thompson. This process took eighteen weeks and involved others on the wing acting as lookouts, which always ran the risk of betrayal. But Moody and Tuite both had reputations that commanded fear. Tuite later said in an interview on Belfast radio, "I think the police did me a favour because they gave me so much bad publicity that the other prisoners really feared me." Others suspected that Moody had a much greater reputation as a hardman.

The intention was to depart their cells on 14 December 1980, but Moody was too large for the hole that led through to Thompson's cell. They had to postpone whilst they worked another day to widen it. The next night, after leaving dummies in their beds, they moved out. Moody managed to get his seventeen-stone body through the first two holes, but then became wedged in the outside wall. He offered to stay, but the others refused and finally pulled him through from the outside. "We literally tore him through the hole. I could hear the muscles tearing right off his back. He left a lot of flesh behind but we got him through," Tuite later recalled.

On the roof they avoided the camera as it automatically swivelled and responded to a light that came on in another cell, as prearranged by the escapees. By the time it reverted to routine they had passed along. They moved around the roof, crossing razor-sharp barbed wire before descending to the ground, using some planks and scaffolding that were lying around before fixing the grapnel and dropping a rope. With the escape postponed by a day, there was no waiting car. However, as they were dressed in their civilian clothes (all three were still awaiting trial, none of them convicted prisoners), they walked away down Lyham Road and found a minicab to take them to Herne Hill. There they were dropped off at one of Moody's friends in order to organise transport to take them out of London, to a bolthole near Canterbury. This was where they were to stay for a short while.

Thompson was the first to leave, after seeing the TV news. He gave himself up because, although he had been in custody for seventeen months, he was due to appear in court the day after his escape. The trial had continued regardless and he had been acquitted in his absence. All he now faced was the charge of escaping custody.

Moody was never recaptured. He lived on for thirteen years, working variously as a hitman or armed robber. Though he supposedly had his freedom, there are times when his life was far from easy. One time, when he was hiding out in a small flat, his family visited him. His son Jason thought, "This was going to be his prison. In some ways it was worse than being in a real prison. Dad felt all the pressure on his shoulders, but he was powerless to help us. It must have driven him crazy. He looked so manic that day. He was so pleased to see us, but I could see in his eyes that he was close to the edge." Moody died in June 1993, when a gunman walked into a bar where he was having a drink and pumped four bullets from a .38 Webley into his chest.

Tuite was later arrested in Ireland. Today he is a businessman, living quietly with his family.

When **Jose Espinosa** and **Otis Blunt** made their exit from the high-security cells of Union County jail, Elizabeth, New Jersey, in December 2007, they left behind a handwritten note (later described as 'sarcastic') that read: "Thank you Officer Zurick for the tools needed. You're a real pal! Happy Holidays." It was accompanied by the smiley face image with which prisoners traditionally embellish their letters. Subsequently, Zurick buckled under the media attention and committed suicide. Both men were arrested a month later, in January; Blunt in a hotel room in Mexico City; Espinosa barely a mile away, in a basement flat. Both may now live to regret the writing of that note.

Their escape had elements of Hollywood about it. They were in adjacent cells, and made a hole to connect them by scraping away the cement around the cinderblock with a thick piece of wire, and then crushing the block with a steel water shut-off wheel, hiding the debris in plastic food containers amongst their possessions in a foot locker. They also made a hole of twenty by forty centimetres and then scraped away in a similar fashion at the outside wall of Espinosa's cell, removing a cinderblock in the same manner. As it took a few days, they concealed their workmanship with pin-ups of bikini-clad girls.

On the night of 15 December, leaving pillows to give the appearance that they were asleep in bed, they wriggled through the hole onto a roof and made a fifteen-foot jump with a thirty-foot drop to get over the razor-wired perimeter fence, landing in a railway easement. After their escape, they went off in different directions according to the tracks left in the snow. No blood was found, and conjecture remains as to whether they took a running jump to make the fifteen feet, or if it was from a standing position. It all sounds like a superhero comic or Hollywood action-adventure – or, at best, a talent for 'parkour', the urban activity that includes extreme acts like leaping from one building to another.

(As might be expected, *The Shawshank Redemption* was the other film referenced in the reports, because of the pin-ups used to cover the holes – though as someone glibly remarked, the pin-ups in the film were better as they included Raquel Welch.)

The previous escape was carried out as quietly as possible, but not so with **Peter Gibb**, helped out of prison by his lover, Heather Parker, who had earlier been one of his guards. Their relationship started in 1988, after she began working in the Melbourne Remand Centre. Their trysts occurred in the honeymoon cells and various cupboards around the building. Gibb was a career criminal, on remand awaiting trial for robbery. Parker stopped working there nine months before his escape.

In March 1993, Parker provided Gibb and another robber, **Archie Butterly**, with plastic explosives needed to blast the window out of their cell, so that they could climb down to the pavement with a rope made from bed-sheets. Parker had arranged for a stolen car to be waiting outside, with a .32 Beretta pistol in the glove compartment. During their escape they crashed the car. Butterly shot and wounded a policeman who tried to intervene. Switching to the police car, they met up with Parker in south Melbourne and all three took to the road. They were found six days later, near the Jamieson River, after a motel at Gaffney's Creek where they had stayed was burned down. There was an exchange of fire between the fleeing group and the police. Gibb and Parker were arrested, but Butterly was shot dead. Conjecture remains as to whether he was killed by the police, by his own hand, or by one of the other two. It has been said that Butterly bore no powder traces from firing guns in that final battle.

Ruby Sparks was semi-legendary in being both the first man to escape from Strangeways, and the first to escape from Dartmoor. When he was imprisoned in Strangeways in 1927, he remarked to his visiting girlfriend that he found neither the jail nor the Manchester air conducive to good health, and that he would have to leave within a fortnight. He was overheard by a guard who told him that no one had ever escaped.

Sparks was true to his word. Within two weeks he had vacated his cell, leaving behind a dummy shape in his bed made from a stool, a chamber pot and a blanket. He had to fashion a suit from another blanket, as his clothes were taken from him each night and left outside his cell, his escape record from borstal preceding him. He had to pay bribes to purchase as much mailbag thread as possible, in order to plait a rope, and also to obtain a knife to saw through the window bars of his cell. His next-door cellmate had pleaded to go with him, and Sparks agreed – though in the event he turned out to be a hindrance, as he was nervous at each step and slowed down the escape.

Prison Break

They had broken into the workshop to make a T-shape from wood as a hook to catch on the spikes. But, as a result of the accompanying escapee's hesitance, Sparks missed his girlfriend, Lily Goldstein ('the Bobbed-Haired Bandit'), who was parked outside the prison with instructions to depart at a certain time. She left only seconds before they came over the wall. Though Sparks and his friend managed to thumb lifts, they became trapped in an orchard where the workers suspected them of stealing the apples, setting about them with stones and pitchforks. The farmhands were so hostile that Sparks was pleased when the police came to their rescue.

After his next conviction for robbery, Sparks had hoped to escape from the truck taking him from the Old Bailey to Wandsworth, as he had secreted a razor blade he intended to use to slash the canvas sides. Goldstein was following in her open-topped Bentley to pick him up, but the warders sat too close to enable him any chance to switch transport.

A subsequent escape attempt from Wandsworth failed, and he was taken to Dartmoor, another prison with no record of successful escapes. Sparks was the first to succeed, remaining out for a hundred and seventy days. But it didn't happen on his first stay, which coincided with the 1932 jail mutiny – which Sparks participated in, receiving a bullet wound in the process.

His escape happened on his next term of residence, which began in 1939. His aim was to acquire five keys to get him through a series of doors. Each time he returned as part of a working party in the quarry, Sparks made sure he was close enough to the officer opening the gates to study and memorise the keys, so that he could scrape away at the metal bits his friend **Alex Marsh** obtained from the machine shop. It took a year of slow work to fashion the keys and test them whenever the chance could be found.

Meanwhile, **Paddy Nolan** was plaiting a rope from mailbag

thread. To obtain finance, Sparks carved some dice – loaded dice, to be specific. It was a risky business cheating his fellow inmates, but, when £3 was accumulated, he felt they were ready for the escape. He chose a Wednesday, when a choral class was held in the prison chapel. Sparks had also arranged for some other inmates to cause a disturbance, and whilst it was being quelled he set off with his two friends through the gates, taking three warders' raincoats in the process and collecting the rope for the wall from under a pile of rubble in the yard.

On that freezing January night in 1940, they escaped onto the moor. They made for the railway track and intended setting off towards London, but went in the wrong direction and almost got caught by the search party. They took refuge in a train wagon and woke up in Plymouth, where they bought some clothes from a pawnbroker. By taking buses until their finances ran low, then slipping on and off trains, avoiding the ticket inspectors, two days later they arrived in London. Sparks remained free for six months before he was recaptured. It would be his last escape.

A most extraordinary escape through the bars occurred in early twentieth-century Germany. **Karl Schaarschmidt** was a repeat escapee, for whom they had to prepare a special cell in Gera Prison, one with thicker masonry and a thicker wooden door, and locks that could not be touched from inside. They also replaced the iron bars on the cell with two wooden bars in the form of a cross, comprising nine-inch and seven-inch-thick oak beams and sunk deep into the masonry. No implements were allowed in the cell. Schaarschmidt was allowed only a pewter spoon to eat with, which was removed after each meal. And yet in 1907, five months after his latest term of imprisonment began, he escaped again, through the window. It wasn't until his recapture two years later that they discovered his method, when they saw his front teeth were worn to the gums. Like a trapped rat, he had gnawed his way through the beams on the window.

There are times when the escape is more mundane than the high adventure of criminal activity, or the desolation of custody. One such case was that of **Oliver Curtis Perry**, who raided trains in such spectacular ways, taking high risks as he hung from the outside or hijacking the train when he was in a corner. After he was sentenced, he was moved from Auburn Prison, New York, to the State Hospital for the Criminally Insane. He also received much female attention. In a bible sent in 1895 by an admirer was a concealed hacksaw blade, which he used to cut through the bars. After releasing other prisoners, he made his escape by sliding down an eighty-foot drainpipe. He was soon recaptured. Imprisonment took its toll, and, in 1920, he made a device with a block of wood and two nails to pierce both his eyes. Blind, he later tried to starve himself to death, but he was force-fed until he died in 1930, not having spoken to either guards or inmates for the previous few years.

Robert Cole used laxatives to escape from his Long Bay prison hospital cell in Sydney, on 18 January 2006. By reducing dramatically by fourteen kilograms from his full bodyweight of seventy within a fortnight, he was able to squeeze his way through the fifteen-centimetre gap between the steel bar of his cell window and the brick wall, which he had widened a little by scraping away with a butter knife over the previous three weeks. No one had noticed how he had shed twenty per cent of his weight in such a short time. Cole had been found not guilty of stealing and assault in November 2003 by reason of mental illness. But he had a string of offences including armed robbery that went back over seventeen years, and there was no date set for his release.

Once he was out of the cell, he still had to scale one fence, then climb another that took him three quarters of the way up a perimeter wall, then walk atop the wall before going over. Blood was found on the ground from a cut sustained from the rolled razor-wire, though he used a blanket to limit the damage. For some reason motion detectors and security cameras did not pick him up. Eleven years before, these measures had been put in place at night to replace guards in the watchtowers. Cole was only out for three days; he was discovered in a shopping mall at Bondi Junction's Oxford Street, accompanied by a woman.

Whilst some escapees have dieted to get through small holes, those who were more bulky often pointed out how their size impeded the escape. The **Marquis de Sade**, imprisoned in the Fort Miolans Prison for sodomy and poisoning four young prostitutes with Spanish Fly during an orgy in June 1772, noted how he discovered a window without bars in a closet adjoining a private dining area he had been allowed to use for his meals. On the evening of 30 April 1773, around 8:30pm, he squeezed through it with two others. Despite his large size, he lowered himself thirteen feet with a sheet, or possibly a small ladder provided by a local farmer who met them and guided them to the French border, and freedom for a year or so. Sade's candle had been left to burn in his cell to delay discovery, along with a letter apologising for his departure, and asking for his effects and other items to be forwarded to his wife.

David McMillan, a drug smuggler from a wealthy background, had entered the drug world for a life of adventure. Today he works as a packer in Surrey, as part of his parole conditions after a heroin bust at Heathrow Airport. He hopes that the extradition laws remain the same, otherwise he will be taken back to Thailand, to the infamous Klong Prem Prison in Bangkok, from whence he escaped in August 1996. He had been waiting for three years for his trial, and an almost certain death sentence for drug smuggling.

Prison Break

Klong Prem is known as a hellhole, or by its ironic nickname, the 'Bangkok Hilton'. Though for McMillan, money had allowed him to live better than most of the others in Building Six, with his own chef, servants and food brought in from the local supermarket, while others rotted away in a world of vermin, worms, tuberculosis and AIDS, barely surviving on soup and the odd fish-head. "I had access to television and radio and my own office, and instead of seventy to a cell we just had five." He was paying for it all, of course. "I did not see it as bribery. The guards saw themselves as helping and I was just showing my gratitude. We wanted it to be a bit more like a hotel and we were willing to pay."

McMillan's way out was to work on the two window bars of his third-floor cell, cutting them with hacksaw blades brought in amongst a box of pornography as a distracting gift for his guards. One night in August 1996, he went through the window and descended forty feet using webbing belts. Once he reached the prison factory, he collected gaffer tape, picture frames, clothes and water. Using the frames and tape to make a ladder with bamboo poles, he scaled two walls and dropped over a further electrified wall before reaching 'Mars Bar Creek', an eight-foot wide moat of raw sewage that he had to wade through. He washed himself with water and changed his clothes, departing concealed beneath an umbrella to shield himself from recognition as the morning guard shift was arriving. When he reached the main road he hailed a taxi. Four hours later he was flying to Singapore, with the new passport his contacts had left for him in Chinatown. He is the first Westerner to have escaped the prison that houses six hundred foreigners amongst its twelve thousand inmates.

Years earlier, in 1983, he had almost made history in Australia when a helicopter escape was prevented by the authorities who had been warned by Lord Tony Moynihan, who had fallen out with

McMillan after failing to trap him in a gambling sting operation. McMillan had paid £250,000 for the escape bid from Pentridge Prison, Melbourne. The plan was to have him flown out and taken in a van to Sydney, where a yacht would have taken him to Manila.

Bank robber **Brenden Abbott,** along with four inmates serving life – **Jason Nixon, Andrew Jeffery, Oliver Alincic** and **Peter Stirling** – broke out of Sir David Longland Correctional Centre at Walcol, near Brisbane, in November 1997. This was a high-security prison that was supposed to be escape-proof. The group, led by Abbott, cut their way free using angel wire smuggled in by a female visitor who secreted it in her vagina. Once they had gone through their cell windows, they passed plastic chairs out to use as a ladder for climbing over the razor-wire that circled the B-block perimeter. From there they moved to the perimeter fences and cut their way through. They were watched by other inmates from their cells, though not one raised the alarm. When three guards arrived on the scene, they were forced to back off by an accomplice's covering gunfire. The escapees left in a waiting getaway car. All were recaptured not long after, except for Abbott, who remained free for six months.

Abbott, dubbed 'the Postcard Bandit', became the subject of a personality cult. For the five and a half years he was on the run from an earlier escape, he supposedly sent the police postcards of himself to taunt them. This never actually happened; it was a propaganda ploy by the police, who came across some photos in a raid that showed Abbott in front of banks he had robbed, and thought it might be a good media device to galvanise the public against him. Instead, it backfired and gave him heroic status.

Annanias Mathe, a Mozambican gang leader (of about forty men) who was awaiting trial on fifty-one charges, including murder, rape and robbery of private houses, escaped from his cell at

Prison Break

C-Max Prison Pretoria, South Africa, in November 2006. He was their first escapee in thirty-six years. Mathe had removed the bullet-proof window using a spoon, and had taken two bars from his bed to help lever himself through a gap of twenty by sixty centimetres. To aid his passage, he spread petroleum jelly on his body – though it's still difficult to believe he managed to get his head through the tiny hole.

With the help of a rope of bedclothes held by another steel bed bar as a hook, he lowered himself down the outside wall, pausing to scrawl with his grimy fingers an endearing "fuck you" to his jailers. He was still wearing leg irons and handcuffs. Though he stole a car in Johannesburg, it was fitted with a tracking device (as are many cars because of the high level of theft) and he abandoned it to continue on foot. Two weeks after his escape, he was caught – not by the police, but by the private security firm who installed the device. They shot him in the buttocks and legs.

There are some escapes which do not succeed in the sense that the escapees are caught inside the prison, rather than a few hours or days later after a bout of temporary freedom. Nevertheless, the description of the escape, its preparations and its setting in motion until that dreaded point when it fails, is part of what we are exploring here. **Norman Parker** has written volumes on his experience of incarceration, one of which details an escape that almost worked. He describes the formidable barriers that have to be overcome, particularly in high-security prisons. The location was Albany Prison on the Isle of Wight. Though undated, the era was probably the 1970's or 1980's.

As Albany is a relatively modern prison, the materials used in the walls were specially-hardened German bricks that are difficult to work through, and the window bars are of tough manganese steel.

The drop to the ground from Parker's cell was about thirty-five feet. The first fence was twenty-four-feet-high, topped with a barbed-wire roll and razor-wire halfway up, with a trembler bell every twenty feet or so. Other obstacles included detectors buried on the path alongside the fence that were sensitive to anyone walking close by, bright lights and CCTV cameras. Then there was the outer fence, with razor-wire halfway up but no wire on top. And even if one made it to the outside world, there was the close proximity of two other prisons – Camp Hill and Parkhurst – which more or less forced one to travel south to escape the island, which would have to be done by boat or by swimming four miles through dangerous currents or a busy shipping lane. It was a formidable set of obstacles.

Parker explains that he could not escape alone; the right partner had to be found, as the twenty-four-foot ladder had to be lifted over the fences, which took two. His idea for making and storing the ladder was novel. Various inmates had made large aviaries in their cells. Not only could a false bottom be built to store sections of a ladder, but the removal of bits of wood would not be too noticeable, as inmates regularly smuggled materials from the workshops for their hobbies and the guards turned a blind eye. Parker's cage, which was over six feet in length, was designed to take six-foot sections of a ladder with three pairs of sleeves to fit the lengths together. As a cover, he acquired a cockatoo that was particularly bad-tempered and would bite any hand that came near it. To keep it company, and to prevent anyone opening the cage, he added a handful of zebra finches that would escape smartly, given the chance.

Parker and his accomplice had a lifeboat station in mind as the place to obtain the transport to take them off the island, or, failing that, they would steal another craft along the coast.

When all was ready, the last act was to remove the bars – which were cut with a carborundum block, a slow process, then filled with

Polyfilla and painted for daytime concealment. As a prisoner had recently been discovered cutting his bars, Parker's accomplice decided that it would be easier to attack the steel frames of his cell door and cut them where the locks slid in, concealing it temporarily with painted cardboard. And so, at 2am one morning, when activities and patrols were at their most minimal, his accomplice broke from his cell by pulling his door inwards, then slipped along to Parker's cell, withdrew the bolt and entered.

Parker had prepared the ladder, much to the disgust of the cockatoo – who was not happy to be disturbed at night. Webbing that had been stolen earlier was attached to the bars that were not cut, and they squeezed through with difficulty. The webbing was elastic, and the downward journey was more hair-raising than Parker had imagined.

When both were down, the ladder lengths were joined and they set off for the fence. What amazed them was that, despite the glare of lights and cameras trained on them, none of the guards noticed. They were undoubtedly dozing. "A brass band could have marched along the fence and they would have missed it."

Unfortunately, another inmate, a 'nonce', had seen them and raised the alarm. Parker slammed the ladder against the first fence "with an impact that must have sent every trembler bell ringing," he admits. The attempt was already spiralling into disaster. Though he was up the rungs as the guards and dogs finally emerged, making it to the top, his pal was brought to ground. Parker hung and kicked out, hoping to fall to the grass safely. It didn't break his ankles, but the jarring landing sprained them. Any attempt at the second fence was doomed. The bid was over.

David McMillan was far from the first to take to a life of crime out of a sense of adventure. **Jacques Mesrine**, whom we met earlier, had been trained by the French military and fought in the

Algerian war. Commended for his bravery, he found that any form of ordinary life afterwards just did not have the appeal or the panache that he craved. The first escape that the French gangster – or 'international criminal', a label he relished – made was in Canada, from the small Percé Prison where he was being held for murder with his lover, **Jeanne Schneider**. What is remarkable is the ease with which he moved around the place, checking out details before going to collect Schneider who was in a cell in the women's block, its only prisoner.

At night there were only three guards in the whole place. Mesrine made himself a knife from the handle of an aluminium mug by sharpening it against the concrete in his cell. On 17 August 1969, when the guard made his rounds, Mesrine jumped up from reading and grabbed the warder, holding a knife to his throat whilst he removed his keys. Locked in the cell, the guard was so afraid that he did not shout for help.

Mesrine could find no other guards around, so he quickly ran through the keys to make sure he had all that were needed for an escape. The first two doors were easy, as was the one into the yard, but he was unsure whether he could open the main door. Once he discovered he had the full set of keys, he went to the women's wing where Schneider had overpowered her guard and was waiting. On the way out they stopped at the kitchen and stocked up with provisions. By the time they were beyond the walls, they heard the alarm sounding. With only two roads out of town, the escapees went up into the wooded mountain slopes around the fishing port. Escape from these surroundings would prove too difficult, and, after going around and around in circles, they were caught.

Mesrine escaped again on 21 August 1972 from the 'escape-proof' maximum-security wing of the Saint Vincent de Paul Prison in Laval, outside Montréal. He took five others with him, crawling through the grass below the fence as they cut through it with pliers. Despite the audacity of such an escape in broad daylight, with guards supposedly watching from the towers, Mesrine wished to further enhance his reputation by returning two weeks later. After three bank jobs to finance his scheme, he intended to free the other fifty-seven people in the maximum-security wing, a number of whom he would provide with rented flats, along with guns for virtually all the others. What Mesrine had not accounted for was the additional security since his own recent escape. The attempted mass breakout, with the support of his accomplice Jean-Paul Mercier, would result in a gun battle with the police and their return to the city empty-handed – even if their insolence had been duly noted, and their credentials moved up the scale a few notches. As a result, the police were given instructions to shoot them on sight in future.

In May 1978, Mesrine was incarcerated back in France and planning to escape from La Santé Prison in Paris, which no prisoner had ever achieved before. To make things even more embarrassing for the authorities, he intended to escape from a top-security wing that had been constructed specifically for him.

In fact the prison knew of his plan. They had received word that Mesrine was going out on 5 May 1978. Nothing happened on that day because it was raining, so the plan was postponed. Then, on 8 May, three of the four prisoners housed in the top-security wing were exercising in the courtyards beside their quarters: **Carman Rives**, a robber and murderer, was in courtyard number nine, whilst **François Besse**, the bank robber, was in number five with Mesrine.

At 9:55am Mesrine had a visit from his lawyer. She waited in an interview room for him to be brought to her, then two guards sat outside watching them through the glass window. At 10am Besse asked to go back to his cell as he was cold. Rives thought something was wrong and asked to go back too.

Mesrine had been discussing with his lawyer one of the Canadian murders that he was to be tried for, now that the French and Canadian authorities had started to cooperate mutually on law enforcement, and asked the guard if he could retrieve the relevant papers from a box in Besse's cell. (What Mesrine's papers should be doing in Besse's cell is a question the guard seems not to have asked.) The guard went to Besse and asked for the papers. Besse tried to hand the box through the bars, but it was too big. The guard had to open the cell door, at which point Besse threw the box and squirted soapy water into his eyes, bringing his knee up into the warder's groin for good measure. The second warder came running and Besse turned to face him.

With no one outside the interview room, Mesrine jumped up on the table. Informing his lawyer that he would prove the room was bugged – thus, perhaps, giving her a cover story for when she was asked why she did not raise the alarm: to which, in fact, she said that it wasn't her job to do so – he deftly removed the cover of a ventilation shaft with some nail scissors, and reached in to withdraw two guns and a length of mountaineering rope with a grappling iron at one end. (These were placed there by a corrupt guard, though it has never been resolved as to whom.)

Mesrine went out into the corridor and rammed his gun into the neck of the guard who was pinning Besse against the wall. Both guards were pushed into Besse's cell and locked in, with their clothes removed. Mesrine and Besse, dressed as guards, made their way down the corridor. As they passed Rives' cell he was invited to join them. In the staff office at the end they found two assistant governors, the chief warder and five others, all of whom they stripped of weapons, keys and any papers that they deemed useful. Rives took one of the uniforms for himself while Mesrine cut the telephone connections. When two nurses arrived unexpectedly, they were locked in a broom cupboard.

Outside the wing, in the yard, they confronted civilian workers and instructed them to bring their ladder through to another courtyard. When they encountered other guards with prisoners they instructed them to join the party, taking them through a door that happened to have been left unlocked. The guard who should have been in the protected sentry box was walking around, smoking. Mesrine took him by surprise, removed his rifle and instructed the guards to erect the ladder against the wall.

Unknown to Mesrine, two of the workers had run back into the main building and were raising the alarm. As armed guards and police rushed to the wall on either side, Besse was up the ladder, fixing the rope and grapple. He was first down. Rives was to go second, but lost his nerve and backed off. Mesrine shot up the ladder and sat on the top of the wall. Bullets started to fly at him. Rives changed his mind again at Mesrine's insistence. Though he followed, he was slow and hesitant. Mesrine fired at the police, and shouted to a woman passing with her pram to move as there was an escape underway. Besse was away and running, whilst Rives was shaking and uncertain. He was still hanging on the rope when a policeman shot him dead. In the meantime, Besse had hijacked a Renault and Mesrine joined him.

By 10:25am, Besse and Mesrine were shooting across the boulevard St Jacques, jumping the red lights on their way. It transpired that, out of twenty prison employees, on that particular day sixteen had not come to work, either suffering from migraine, overwork or marital problems. Further, when they reached into the ventilation shaft that Mesrine had used as his store, they also produced two more revolvers, two knives, a hand-grenade and a fuse for a bomb.

While all of Paris panicked, Mesrine was having a bath in a safe-house apartment, asking its owner politely if he could use the Floris bath essence – and later returning his host's courtesy by insisting it was his turn to do the washing-up after dinner. As he would have wanted it, media portrayals tended to glorify him. To quote his biographer, Carey Schofield, "To the end of his life he retained the vulnerability of an insecure young actress in fear of bad press reviews."

The **Biddle Brothers** escaped from prison sixteen days prior to their execution. Their story was told in a theatrical piece that played for many years, and later became the basis of a film, *Mrs Soffel*, starring Mel Gibson and Diane Keaton, some of which was filmed in the original jail.

Ed and Jack Biddle escaped on 30 January 1902, from Allegheny County Jail in Pennsylvania, with the help of an insider, Katherine Soffel, the wife of the prison governor. Once it was announced they were to die, she had visited the brothers to bring them the consolation of religion, but had fallen in love with Ed Biddle. Then she brought them guns and hacksaw blades.

They occupied adjoining cells on the second floor. Just before 4am, one of them called the night guard and asked for some medicine for his brother, who was sick. When the guard arrived, Jack sprang through the opening in the cell door that he had cut away, seized the guard around the waist and hurled him over the railing to the stone floor some sixteen feet below. Ed joined him and they went down to the first floor where they met the second guard, whom they shot. The guard on the third floor was ordered down, and all three of them locked in the dungeon. The brothers took the keys, went to the locker room and changed into suits. It seems they then met up with Mrs Soffel, and went out through her home into a snowbound Ross Street. She went with them. She had drugged her husband to make sure he did not wake, and had arranged for their four children to be away that night.

When the morning guards came in at 6am, they discovered the

escape and raised the alarm. It appears the escapees had taken a trolley to West View, according to some reports, but others state that a carriage had been organised by Mrs Soffel. Out of town, they walked along Route 19 for a mile until they found a farm where they could steal a horse and sleigh, as the snow there was more hazardous. As they headed north into Butler County, a posse soon caught up with them. In the resulting gun battle, Jack was killed and Ed injured. Soffel asked Ed to shoot her, rather than for her to be captured. He complied, before dying himself. Soffel survived and was later incarcerated in Allegheny County Jail. Her husband resigned and moved away with their children.

John Dillinger was the most famous gangster of his day, his fame resting on events within an eleven-month period from September 1933 to July 1934. One of these events was his escape on 3 March 1934 from the 'escape-proof' Lake County jail in Crown Point, Indiana. In fact, the authorities were so confident that it was secure that any attempt to move him elsewhere because of a delay in his trial was thwarted. They would live to regret the decision.

What gained so much press attention was that Dillinger escaped using a fake gun, whittled out of wood and then blackened with shoe polish. Whether this was true or not is contentious. Perhaps it was a real gun, or a wooden gun smuggled in. It is also suspected that Dillinger's lawyer, Louis Piquette, had bought off a judge who then smuggled a gun into the jail. This did not become public until after both Dillinger and the judge had died, but the fake gun story sounds better. Sometimes one has to take heed of the remark in John Ford's film, *The Man Who Shot Liberty Valance*: "When the legend becomes fact, print the legend."

In any case, at 9am Dillinger started using the gun to methodically capture and lock up a series of trusties, a jail attendant, a deputy sheriff and a prison warden, each time obtaining further information vital to his escape. Needing to increase his arsenal, Dillinger took two Thompson submachine guns from the warden's office. From there he returned to the cells and asked if anyone wished to make the escape with him. **Herbert Youngblood,** a black man on a murder charge, accepted the offer and was handed a submachine gun. Two others agreed and the group set off for the garage at the rear of the prison. Three vigilante farmers who were there to guard the prisoners were taken and locked in a washroom, along with the two other would-be escapees who suddenly got cold feet. Others were rounded up in the garage, including prison kitchen workers and various trusties. Whilst Youngblood stood guard over them, Dillinger looked for a suitable car for their getaway. The garage mechanic told him the sheriff's car was the fastest, so Dillinger decommissioned all the others, yanking out their ignition wires, and they took the sheriff's car, with the mechanic and the deputy as hostages.

Once out of town, without a shot ever being fired, the deputy and the mechanic were ushered out of the car and given their fare to return to town. Dillinger's mistake was to take the sheriff's car across state lines into Illinois, violating a federal law that allowed the FBI to join in the manhunt.

Youngblood was killed thirteen days later in a shootout in Michigan. As he lay dying he indicated that Dillinger had been with him the day before, triggering a manhunt in that state and over the border in Canada. Dillinger was in fact a long way away, holed up in luxury in St Paul, Minnesota with his girlfriend, Billie Frechette.

Dillinger's method of escaping with smuggled guns dates back to a breakout he organised in Michigan City State Prison for a group of bank robbers, led by **Harry Pierpont**, who he met there during an earlier sentence. As Dillinger was released first, in May 1933, he vowed to raise funds and organise their mass escape. A package of guns and bullets was thrown over the wall at a point where an arrow was painted on the prison shirt factory. It was retrieved early next morning by an inmate and hidden in shirt fabric in the warehouse. It was a month before either the weapons or ammunition were used. The escapees had intended to take the parole board hostage, but that visit occurred on a day when the prisoners were scattered around doing different jobs.

On 26 September 1933 Pierpoint and nine others escaped from the prison, when they took hostage the assistant deputy superintendent and the shirt factory superintendent by luring them to the basement of the factory. With these two hostages, the men walked the entire length of the penitentiary with guns concealed beneath the shirts they carried in their arms. No guards or prisoners gave them more than a cursory glance, believing they were going about ordinary prison business. Only when they reached the fence gate did the hostages tell the guard quietly about the situation and request that the gate be opened. As they went through that gate and the next, each successive guard was made to join the entourage. At one point a guard refused to open the gate – with a few thrusts of a steel shaft the lock was shattered, and the guard knocked unconscious for his delaying tactics. Once they reached the administrative building, they had to herd all the clerks into a vault, break the telephone lines and raid the prison arsenal. The warden too stumbled into the breakout, and was detained. Outside they split up, with each group taking off in a number of hijacked cars.

On the night before their mass escape, Dillinger himself had been captured at the home of a new female infatuation. The Pierpoint gang understood immediately that they now had to break him free. They walked into the jail in Lima, Ohio, on 12 October and announced they were officers from Indiana, come to take Dillinger to Michigan City. The sheriff asked to see their credentials and, when their guns appeared, made for his holster on the wall, only to be shot down.

In May 1984, six men on death row escaped together from the Mecklenburg Correctional Center in Boydton, Virginia. **James** and **Linwood Briley, Lem Tuggle, Earl Clanton, Derick Peterson** and **Willie Jones** took advantage of the lax procedures of the prison officers. Clanton had hid unnoticed in an officer's restroom on being returned from evening recreation. He charged out when another inmate signalled that the door was open and released the locks in the unit, allowing the inmates to start a takeover. As they captured each of the officers, they locked them up and stole their uniforms. Finding riot gear in a closet, they donned helmets and shields and draped gasmasks around their necks. A nurse who had been giving out medication was saved from rape and probable injury by one of the inmates, who chose to stay behind.

Their ruse to escape was a fake bomb – which was in fact the prisoners' TV set with a blanket thrown over it, carried on a green canvas stretcher – which they sprayed with a fire extinguisher at a strategic moment as they marched out of the unit. Their decoy was then placed in a van with them and driven from the prison. It was all just implausible enough to catch the guards unawares. Once they were through the gates, they radioed back to the control tower: "Secure the sally port gates." They had escaped.

But, as with so many breakouts, there were no further plans. All they had was some money, almost $800 removed from the pockets of the officers' uniforms. The first to be caught were Clanton and Peterson, who were found the next day intoxicated in a Laundromat, still wearing the uniforms but with the badges torn off. Everyone was recaptured within eighteen days, and eventually executed.

Catching the guards off-guard by doing something unexpected was ably demonstrated by **Coelius Secundus Curion**, a cleric who made his escape from prison in Turin during the seventeenth century with a clever ploy. Chained to a large piece of wood by both feet, he asked his warder if one leg could be freed for a day as it was uncomfortable. The warder obliged. Curion then set about fashioning a dummy leg by stuffing his shirt into the legging whilst sitting on his good leg. It seems it was convincing enough, for the next day he asked the warder to re-chain one leg and release the other. After the warder had departed, Curion was able to stand free of the restraints. As no prisoner was expected to slip his chains there were not many guards in the prison, so Curion left through the window and over the wall.

Mark DeFriest has made a career out of escaping in the State of Florida. His initial term of imprisonment (which was a dubious charge in the first place) started in 1980, setting him on a course where he has accumulated so many years for his subsequent escapades that he now seems to be stuck inside for life – a life that might be shorter than anticipated, given that he (and others) witnessed the killing of another prisoner, Frank Valdez, allegedly by guards in 1999. Since then, with the guards on trial, DeFriest and the other witnesses have made allegations about beatings and death threats.

DeFriest states that the best way to achieve an escape is to have money. Money was obtained at one point by producing a public newsletter, asking for funds to be paid into his bank accounts around the USA. Another method was by running an in-house drug business. With money you can buy anything and anyone, particularly guards who will supply you with whatever you need.

Thus, for many years, DeFriest acquired the tools he needed to get out of his cell. He became so adept at adapting and making things that he wasn't even allowed a toothbrush, as he could fashion a key from one. He boasted that, no matter how much they stripped back his cell, he would always find a way to escape. In one search of his cell, when nothing was found, he boastfully pointed to a slight slit above the cell door and, using a piece of wire, fished out a key made from a toothbrush.

One of his regular methods was to conceal tools and implements within a 'charger', a six-inch aluminium tube secreted up the anus. One time it was noted that the charger DeFriest was using contained "thirty-four razor blades, seven hacksaws, six handcuff keys, solder, drill bits and padlock keys, twenty hundred-dollar bills, $19 in postage, gold jewellery and a set of keys with interchangeable teeth". Consequently, he was regarded as able to escape from any institution. At one prison the restrictions were so tight that they built a special cell for him, reminding one of the fictional serial killer Hannibal Lecter.

At Bay County Prison, where DeFriest made half a dozen escape attempts and dismantled three cells with a toothbrush, they suggested that the guards might quit if he returned. As with other escapees, he has sawn through bars, climbed down knotted bed sheets and crawled over chain-link fences. But it is keys that are his forte, which he can seemingly fashion out of anything. And there seems little worth in handcuffing him, for he has been known to reduce them to scraps of metal within minutes. His first ever escape in prison was made by dismantling a cell door, and rolling it back with his hands: "The door was kind of like a can of sardines."

Today, given his position as witness to the murder of an inmate, he seems to have stopped trying to escape. Indeed, his current prison conditions might make it easier than on many previous occasions. But he also knows that, if he is caught escaping, they may not hesitate to pull the trigger.

Robert Latimer was jailed in 1889 after bungling the murder of his mother. He then managed to fumble another crime, this time within prison walls. By 1893 he was a trusty in Michigan State Prison and put in charge of the prison pharmacy. One night in

March he served sardines and lemonade to a couple of guards, to which he added liberal doses of prussic acid and opium. Within twenty minutes one guard was dead, the other unconscious.

Latimer escaped and turned up on the doorstep of relatives, but they turned him away. When he was recaptured he insisted it had all been a mistake, he had not intended to kill the guard but had added too much prussic acid.

Over the subsequent years, Latimer became institutionalised. When they wanted to abandon the old prison, he refused to move. His cell, with its desk, books and plants, was his home. As he was not considered a danger they let him stay, making him the watchman of the deserted prison. However, a few years later, in 1935, he was forced to leave after forty-six years of incarceration. He became a vagrant until housed in a state home, where he died in 1946, aged eighty.

The case of **Joan Little** is another that contains all manner of other issues besides escape. Little, an African-American woman, was in Beaufort County Jail in Washington, North Carolina, for breaking and entering, larceny and receiving stolen property, when she was accused of the murder of a white prison guard. Clarence Alligood's body was found on her bunk in her cell, naked from the waist downwards. He had been stabbed eleven times with an ice-pick to his head and heart, and semen was discovered on his leg. Little had vanished from the cell. This was in August 1974, at a time when the issues of civil rights, feminism and opposition to capital punishment were all on the agenda. A defence fund and much publicity were forthcoming, and the best lawyers retained.

Little stated that Alligood came to her cell seeking sex three times, between 10pm and 3am. After the first refusal, he returned with cigarettes and sandwiches as bribes. She refused once more. Again he returned later. "I had changed into my nightgown. He was telling me I really looked nice in my gown, and he wanted to have sex with me."

He took off his trousers and shoes and left them in the corridor, entering the cell with a grin. "He said he had been nice to me, and it was time I was nice to him. I told him I didn't feel like I should be nice to him that way." She explained that he fondled her and removed her gown. "That's when I noticed he had the ice-pick in his hand."

Alligood then dragged her to the floor, held the ice-pick to her face and forced her to perform oral sex. She didn't know whether he would kill her or not. During the crucial moments of the sex act, as he loosened his grip on the pick, Little grabbed it and hit him. He lunged at her. "Each time he came, I struck at him. He grabbed me by the wrists, then he was behind me. I put my feet against the bunk to place my weight against him. I hit him over my right shoulder. He fell middleway on the bunk forward, his head facing the wall, his knees on the floor."

Angela Davis, the black social activist, pointed out some questions relating to the case in a lengthy essay: Why was she the only female in the jail – whether prisoner or guard – and a black one at that? Why was a closed circuit television camera pointed at her cell, so that she had no privacy when she dressed or attended to her ablutions? What was the guard doing with an ice-pick in his desk drawer, let alone in her cell?

Little briefly made her escape after killing the guard. She handed herself in to the authorities a week or so later, stating that she had been defending herself against sexual assault. The prosecution at the trial claimed she had seduced Alligood to gain her freedom. She was acquitted, but still had further time to serve plus a further sentence for escaping. Later, with only a month left before being eligible for parole, she escaped again, fleeing to New York where she obtained work at the National Council for Black Lawyers. She was later extradited to North Carolina, and eventually paroled, enabling her to move back to New York to work in the office of a law firm.

Prison Break

When **Hugo Grotius** was sentenced to life imprisonment at Loevestein Castle in the Netherlands in 1619, for treason in connection with religious disagreements between Protestant factions, this political philosopher continued with his life of study and writing. But he is best remembered for escaping. With the flow of books in and out of his cell, his wife arranged for a large chest to be taken in to carry a large consignment out (her husband amongst it). He escaped in 1621, carried out by two soldiers who were supposed to be guarding him. To hinder the discovery his wife told them that he was infectiously ill, keeping them away from the room for some while. He was taken by boat to Gorkum, then by horseback to a friend's home, where the chest was unlocked and he fled via Belgium to Paris. He remained in exile with his wife and daughter for ten years. The original chest can be seen in the Rijksmuseum in Amsterdam, and also in the museum Het Prinsenhof in Delft – though only one can be authentic, obviously.

There was a period extending from the late eighteenth into the nineteenth century when the dilapidated warships at Woolwich and Chatham, commonly called 'the Hulks', were used to house convicts, often awaiting transportation to Australia. It was not impossible to escape, although they could not swim to shore as they were clad in chains and leg irons. Instead, they had to escape onto boats that came up alongside them, overpowering the officers and stealing their weapons in case of an eventual fire-fight. There was a tendency to take the boats south of the river, rather than towards the north banks of the Thames, which were mainly desolate marshlands. If you were caught, you were more likely to be hanged.

During the Northern Irish Troubles, for a short period internment without trial took place on board HMS Maidstone, moored in Belfast Lough. Inevitably an escape occurred in the ice-cold waters, during January 1972. On that foggy night, seven IRA men – **Tucker Kane, Tommy Toland, Tommy Gorman, Jim Bryson, Sean Convery, Peter Rodgers** and **Martin Taylor** – escaped by covering their bodies in grease and swimming ashore. They went after the 4pm headcount, though, due to a miscount, and a recount, they left later than intended.

It was just getting dark. They had prepared for the freezing cold by taking cold showers. A porthole bar had been cut, and they were covered in Echo margarine and boot polish, stripped to their underpants with socks on their hands and feet. After wriggling through the hole, they slid down the hanging hawser till they reached the water. To avoid being seen, they tried to stay underwater as much as possible, swimming breaststroke to avoid splashing. It was five hundred yards across to the Harland and Wolff shipyard. The plan was that they would be met by an armed IRA unit from Andersonstown, but they were nowhere in sight.

And so the group hijacked a bus intended for collecting shipyard workers on overtime. The commotion of the hijack attracted the attention of security guards and precipitated a mad chase as the bus swayed back and forth across the road and the pursuing RUC van tried to overtake them. When they arrived in what was called the Markets area, where they had many supporters, they bunked out into a pub. Dirty and half-naked (or totally naked in some cases), the men were quickly clothed and taken to safe-houses. Some days later they were spirited across the border to reappear at a press conference as 'the Magnificent Seven'.

Isolation surrounded by water was the basis of two other prison systems, the first being the infamous Devil's Island, off the coast of French Guiana in South America. Though Devil's Island was, as the name suggests, a desolate outcrop, the name is usually applied to the whole of the French penal colony system. There was a group of islands offshore, as well as camps on the mainland, one beside Cayenne, the capital on the coast, another deep in the jungle and one more on the river that divided French and Dutch Guiana.

Devil's Island itself was undoubtedly the worst place to be incarcerated. The colony was used by France as a way to rid itself of its worst criminals, in the hope that they would never appear on home territory again. For even when a prisoner had served his sentence he wasn't allowed to return to France, but was released into the colony and given the chance to start a new life in terrain barely habitable for most Europeans. Of course, if a prisoner escaped then no one was going to stop him making his way back to France. But first, of course, he actually had to succeed in escaping. Few managed it, and those who did rarely arrived at a destination of safety. To perish in the process was the usual fate of the escapee.

There are three cases outlined here in chronological order, to chart how circumstances changed over the course of a few years. When the American bank robber **Eddie Guerin** was caught after a robbery at American Express in rue Scribe, Paris, in 1901, he had already served a French term of imprisonment. This time, his sentence was to be life on Devil's Island.

A good proportion of those transported across the Atlantic never arrived, the ships being notoriously unhealthy, with little food or water to keep the prisoners alive. If you were fortunate enough to arrive, you could be assured that no one else would travel across to rescue you. You had to organise your own escape. Those who attempted it by boat mainly failed, and recapture only added years to a sentence, as well as the added burden of dragging a fourteen-pound chain riveted to their legs. Another hindrance was diseases like malaria or scurvy, or bites from the clouds of mosquitoes – let alone the generally overpowering heat and humidity. "Nobody had sufficient energy to lift a hand beyond what was absolutely necessary," Guerin wrote later in his memoir, *I Was a Bandit*.

Guerin had been on one of the islands for a year before being transferred to a camp on the mainland. He was determined to leave. Escape was a challenge he needed, even if he knew his chances of survival would be minimal. The people who lived in the mangrove swamps were likely to murder an escapee, and it was said that those who had escaped together had resorted to cannibalism to survive. None of which even took into account the alligators to be negotiated along the rivers – or indeed the bounty hunters in neighbouring Dutch Guiana, where escapees always headed.

Money could be helpful to bribe the guards, but it was jealously guarded within a 'charger' pushed into the anus. Guerin wrote to his connections back home in America and slowly accumulated some cash. His chance to escape came during the fifth year of his sentence. He was sewing prison clothes on the porch of a building in the camp of Maroni when his thimble fell off, as it did periodically, and the guards gave him permission to climb down and retrieve it from beneath the building. On this particular day, he failed to reappear.

His departure had been arranged with a Belgian who had lived in the countryside and had the skills necessary to handle the terrain, whether it was the undergrowth and swamps, or the excess of insects, rats and other vermin. Money now became essential, as they had to pay the ferryman who took them across the river to Dutch Guiana. For two weeks the pair fought their way through the marshes and creeks, their clothes in tatters. "Daily we got soaked from head to foot fording waterlogged wastes." At night they constructed a bivouac and lay in fear, "while the wild animals of the forest came sniffing around." Gigantic snakes struck at them. "Unkempt and unshaven, our feet a mass of blisters, starving but for the tropical fruit we could pick," Guerin claimed it was a miracle that they found their way out.

Eventually they reached Paramaribo, the capital of Dutch Guiana.

Fortunately, Guerin found a Scotsman who helped him to purchase a white cotton suit, so that he could move around the streets less conspicuously. Though he still looked in a sorry state, covered in bites, he approached the United States Consul. This man helped him to reach his contacts in Chicago and prepare the next step. He even paid for Guerin to stay at the same hotel as himself.

Once it was time to leave, Guerin set off for Georgetown in British Guiana, his passage paid. From there he took a boat, *The City of Quebec*, but, not having enough money left, he had to travel with black people who treated him with contempt, whilst above, "in the saloon were my own race going about in lordly ease." Finally he arrived in New York, the city he had not seen since his departure for Europe, twenty years earlier.

It had been no mean feat to escape Devil's Island, though he remained a fugitive and the French would recapture him if they could. But he was not in hiding. He moved around his hometown of Chicago fairly freely, making the French more determined to arrest and extradite him. The Chicago police were far from keen, forcing the French Consul to contract the Pinkerton Detective Agency to pick him up, by trailing his sister. The French messed up the operation, however, as Billy Pinkerton was sympathetic towards the local boy. On top of that, they had no budget to pay his detectives.

Nevertheless, Guerin took heed of the warning and left the country, crossing back across the Atlantic to England – where by chance he met Chicago May, his former partner, the woman with whom he had been arrested in Paris. May had always done well for herself, earlier earning her living as a 'badger', a prostitute who robbed, blackmailed and fleeced her rich clients.

But some say that Devil's Island had changed Guerin and their relationship no longer showed any spark. He went off with a younger woman and, in her jealousy, May hired a hitman who hunted him down. Guerin survived the bullet, though Chicago May and her accomplice were sent to prison.

The Frenchman **René Belbenoit** was transported to Devil's Island in 1920 for stealing pearls from his employer. He was sentenced to eight years of hard labour. At that time, the conditions of the sentence remained the same: if you were lucky enough to survive the conditions of the penal colony, you would only be released from prison, not brought back home. You were supposed to stay for the same period as your sentence – or, if it ran to more than eight years, you were exiled for life. Thus you would probably have to live in squalid, inhospitable conditions until your death, your punishment becoming effectively a life sentence.

Belbenoit had served with distinction in World War One, and thus was allowed to avoid the hardest labour. But the whole place was disease- and mosquito-infested, and the heat unbearable. If not working in water up to your waist, then you were working naked except for shoes and a straw hat, which helped to minimise escapes. Nevertheless, people did at least try.

Within two weeks, Belbenoit and another man made an escape attempt on a raft, heading for Dutch Guiana. They were caught and returned. A further attempt alongside some others ended in their canoe capsizing on the Maroni River, whereupon they fled into the jungle. They were lucky to climb out of the river, for stories abounded of onlookers watching bodies ripped apart by piranhas, only the skeletons remaining. The jungles were little better, for armies of large soldier ants might also pick you clean. After three escapees died, Belbenoit and the others sought the help of the Indians, who took them to the Dutch – who in turn handed them back to the French.

In 1934, Belbenoit was officially released but wasn't allowed to go back to France. He thought he might try to 'escape' his freedom in the colony and reach the United States. With money given by an American filmmaker who was researching prisons, he bought a boat and set off by sea with five others. They argued during the rough journey and, at one point, Belbenoit had to draw a gun to force everyone to continue.

When they came to Trinidad, the British authorities refused to hand them over to the French, though they were told to set sail again. Their next landing, after sixteen days at sea, was on a beach in Colombia. His companions were apprehended and handed to the French, but Belbenoit was able to exploit some sympathy, escaping again and travelling north. He worked his way slowly through Panama, and up through Central America, until he arrived in California in 1937, carrying the manuscript of a memoir of his trials and tribulations, *Dry Guillotine*. It was a success on publication, but it also attracted the attention of the immigration authorities. He was allowed to stay temporarily, but then told to leave in 1941. After a spell in Mexico, he sought readmission but was caught and imprisoned. Eventually, he gained a passport and went to work in Hollywood, as an advisor at Warner Bros studios.

The third escapee, **Henri Charrière** – better known as **'Papillon'**, derived from the butterfly tattoo on his chest – also recounted his exploits in a book, which was produced as a film in 1973 with Steve McQueen and Dustin Hoffmann. It would grant him a heroic stature, and make Devil's Island infamous.

Papillon was a crook, but was wrongfully condemned to the island for the 1931 murder of a pimp in Paris. No sooner had he arrived than he knew he had to leave. He also knew he would stand a better chance of escaping from the mainland than from one of the three islands that comprised the penal colony. He claimed to be ill and was sent to the mainland hospital, where he escaped by knocking out the guards with the feet of his bed and climbing a wall. With two others, he set off by sailboat – but it turned out to be a rotten vessel, so they ventured into the jungle and found a leper colony, where they bought a better boat with the money Charrière stored in a charger.

They went with the current of the Cayenne river into the Atlantic Ocean, and then sailed north-westerly hoping to find Venezuela. Their first stop was in Trinidad, where the British welcomed them but gave them only two weeks before they had to set off again. Their next stop was Curaçao, where they were shipwrecked and imprisoned. Charrière recounts how he escaped once again by sawing through the bars with hacksaw blades he had bought. From there he fled to the safety of an Indian tribe, where he was allowed to settle for six months. However, he was distracted by his obsession with vengeance against those in Paris who had wronged him in the first place, leading to his recapture and imprisonment. Further escape attempts were made, including smuggling in dynamite in a loaf of bread. All failed, and they were returned to French Guiana at the end of October 1934.

This time, Charrière was placed in solitary confinement for two years on the islands. When World War Two broke out the conditions tightened further, and all escape attempts were punishable by death – unless you were regarded as mad, for then you were no longer responsible for your actions.

Determined to escape, Papillon feigned madness and was sent to the asylum for a while. Later claiming to be cured, he asked to be sent to Devil's Island itself. Wanting to make one last attempt at escape with a raft, he had decided he would rather perish than live any longer in the penal colony. Pondering the impossibility of his predicament and the roughness of the sea, he would sit on the beaches, watching the waves come in and out. Then, one day, he found a place where the waves broke against the rocks differently. The area was not watched by the guards. "This side of the island was completely safe – no one would ever imagine a man would choose the most exposed and therefore the most dangerous place for getting away."

Collecting jute bags to fill with coconuts, he and a companion made two rafts and leapt into the sea at night, on a full moon when the tide was highest, to catch the seventh wave – the large roller that started three hundred yards back and which, after its crash between the rocks, sucked everything back out of the grasp of the next six waves coming in. Their intention was to be swept to sea and carried along for a few days, in the hope of washing up on the mainland. It took forty hours before they came ashore, sunburnt, lips cracked, eyes glued together, altogether in a poor state. Charrière watched his friend, some distance away on his raft, becoming impatient. Despite being warned, he was tempted to step into the shallow water, only to be sucked into quicksand. Charrière kept his patience until he was washed right ashore.

Charrière then went in search of a Chinese man, the brother of a friend on Devil's Island, and together they bought a boat and set sail for Georgetown, navigating by the sun, moon and stars. Though they would be allowed to stay in the British territory, they decided to venture onwards to Venezuela, where, in 1945, Charrière was given citizenship. When he came across *L'Astragale* by Albertine Sarrazin, in a French bookshop, in which the author recounts her prison exploits, he too decided to write his autobiography in the style of a novel.

Though there is nothing to compare to the horrors of Devil's Island, it would seem that Alcatraz also struck fear into the minds of prisoners with the idea of its inescapability. The records show – if they are correct, having been written inside the institution subject to any changes or cover-ups required – that fourteen attempts were made to escape from this island prison in the middle of San Francisco Bay in its twenty-nine years as a federal penitentiary, and that none were successful. Of course, that assumes that the thirteenth attempt, the one that we shall outline, did not succeed. Yet, given that no bodies were ever recovered, and none of the escapees were officially noted as ever having been seen again, it is an assumption that many are not willing to accept.

The first desperate attempt occurred in April 1936 and was made by **Joseph Bowers**. Bowers had no greater plan than just to plunge into the water and do his best to swim or drift to the mainland, unmindful that the currents, let alone the ice-cold water, were said to be enough to kill all but the superhuman. But Bowers never had the chance to put it to the test, for he was shot by a guard in a watchtower as he climbed a chain-link fence.

The second attempt, in December 1937 by **Theodore Cole** and **Ralph Roe**, had more potential, as they fled undercover of fog, making it difficult for the guards to detect their flight. Indeed, there is the possibility that they made it, though the consensus is that they could not have survived the adverse weather conditions. But officialdom must have seriously considered the possibility, for they were placed on the FBI's 'Most Wanted' list.

But if we go through the list of other attempts, the escapes from cells or other buildings around the prison, whether by sawing through bars or walking out, all of them led to detection by guards either on the roofs or across the fences, or by the shore just as the escapees were ready to plunge in, or to push makeshift rafts into the water. They were then mostly fired upon, some being killed, others injured.

John Bayless, the sixth attempted escapee, did manage to start swimming, but gave up. **James Boarman**, one of the four who made their escape in April 1943, was shot whilst swimming, though his body was never recovered. He and his comrades had jumped thirty feet off a cliff into the water in their underwear, their bodies covered in grease. **Floyd Hamilton**, another who took the plunge, managed to return to the shore, eluding capture and remaining, frozen, in a small cave for three days, before climbing back up the cliff and in through the same window he used to escape from the prison. He was discovered beneath a pile of material in a storeroom of the industries area.

John Giles tried to escape in July 1946 by donning the uniform of a US Army staff sergeant and boarding the prison launch. He had gathered together the uniform piece by piece over a number of years, until he had the full costume. He was discovered missing not long after the launch departed, and was met by prison officers at Angel Island.

It appears that only **John Paul Scott**, who escaped in December 1962 with **Darl Parker**, officially managed to make it to the mainland. Theirs was the fourteenth and last attempt. Scott was found on Fort Point suffering from hypothermia. They had used inflated surgical gloves as water wings, their escape starting in the kitchen where they both worked. Noticing that a storeroom could not be seen from a watchtower, they sawed through a bar using moistened string dipped in abrasive kitchen cleaner. It took weeks to accomplish, and was made all the harder because the window was ten feet from the floor. The advantage was that the guards did not check the window for that very reason.

On 2 May 1946, there was an attempt which became known as 'the Battle of Alcatraz', when prisoners took the main cell-house and grabbed two firearms there. They had also intended to take keys to a door, but they were not in their place as a prison officer had breached regulations and not returned them. Thus their attempt was inadvertently blocked. The prisoners refused to surrender and, in the battle that ensued, three of their number and two of the guards were killed.

This sets the scene for the only known escape that may possibly have succeeded – the *Escape from Alcatraz*, as the film based upon it is entitled. On 11 June 1962, **Clarence Anglin**, **John Anglin** and **Frank Morris** made the most elaborately well-planned attempt that we know about. The escape plan was hatched in December 1961 when **Allen West**, a member of the team who failed to go on the night itself, discovered some old hacksaw blades in a utility corridor whilst cleaning. Initially, each started work digging around the vent-holes in their cells, using spoon handles to scrape and scratch (and, later, an electric drill they made from a discarded vacuum cleaner motor and electric hair clippers), digging into the moisture-damaged concrete which broke away quite easily in places. These holes made their way into the utility corridor, an otherwise empty space filled with pipes.

The use of the motor was masked by music played during recreation hour. They also blocked the hole each day with false walls made from *papier mâché* and the canvas boards used for painting, which most of them did as a hobby. One would work while the other kept lookout, using mirrors. They worked from the 5:30pm count until the lights-out count at 9pm. What seems remarkable in this case – as indeed it is in other cases where tunnelling and filing took place – is that no one heard the sounds. Despite the covering music, it has been noted that every single sound was very clearly amplified in Alcatraz, and guards or inmates would prick up their ears instantly if they heard something out of the ordinary. "Almost any sound inside the cell house echoed and reverberated as though the entire building were a drum. Even well-muffled sounds of digging or scratching or filing could not be entirely eliminated," wrote Don DeNevi in *Riddle of the Rock*.

Then they worked on the vent at the top of the cell block, climbing up the three tiers using the pipes as their ladder. Their breakout was prepared over the space of several months, thus the chance of discovery was greater. Bars were regularly given the shakedown, hit with a rubber mallet to see if they rang the same for each. (If they are cut, the sound changes.) But it seems no one checked the air vents at the back of the cells, or indeed the roof vents, very often.

To work on the escape at the top of the third tier of the cell house, which could be viewed by the guard post, West obtained permission to clean it. Because he made dust fall down to the main floor of the cells, he was allowed to hang blankets whilst he worked up there, almost sealing the whole area from prying eyes. The officials were not to know that Morris and the others were also working by night on the air vent, prior to constructing their rafts.

At the same time, they prepared the dummies they would need to leave in their bunks on the night of the escape, or indeed on those evenings they were busy working on the top of the third tier. The *papier mâché* heads were made from toilet paper, soap and cement powder, coloured with paint from the art block and hair from the barber shop. All were hidden by day on the top of the cellblock.

They knew that to get away across the water they needed a raft, as previous attempts had indicated it was too cold to swim. They collected together standard, olive, rubberised-fabric, US Army raincoats that were issued to all the prisoners. They used somewhere in the region of thirty coats, collected from other prisoners or obtained over a period by asking the guards for new ones. These were glued together in such a way that they could be inflated with air. They also made lifejackets for each escapee to wear. To inflate them they would need a bellows – or in this case a concertina, which they obtained via a mail-order catalogue, discarding its sound keys.

Thus, at 9:30pm on that June 1962 night, after lights-out, three men went through their cell holes. Allen West was left behind because his false wall would not stay in place, and he had cemented it in too well. It had hardened and, though one of the others tried to kick it free from the other side, it would not move. West had never actually gone through his hole before, because he was making paddles and lifejackets from the raincoats in his cell. He stated that he did eventually break through after he worked on an unforeseen metal obstacle in the fabric of the wall, but by the time he reached the roof the others were gone. He could not continue alone to the shore as a guard was now watching over one of the vital areas.

The others had gone onto the roof via the prepared vent bars and the ventilator shaft. They had cut the rivets with carborundum cord earlier, replacing them temporarily with little balls of soap. After they ran along the roof for one hundred feet, they went down the old bakery flue to the ground, lowering all their equipment with wire. Then they went over a chain-link fence, dropping down the steep, brush-covered embankment to the shore. They were carrying all their equipment in parts that were then assembled, before blowing up the pontoon-style raft with the makeshift bellows. The raft measured six by fourteen feet, but they dismantled part of it and left it behind for West in case he should follow. It was also noted that they had a reflector and homemade torch with them.

The three prisoners are still officially listed as missing, presumed drowned. The assumption is based on bits of raft, paddles and papers that were found in the water and the vicinity over a period of time. But the authorities found no bodies.

Various possibilities have been suggested about plans they had to get to Angel Island, and then to make their way from there. Some believed that, once they reached the mainland, they would be picked up by a contact, while others said they would steal a car and pull a robbery to obtain the money to keep travelling. Another story claims that, with the help of another resident of Alcatraz, the black gang boss Bumpy Johnson, they were to be picked up just a few hundred yards away. Indeed, given that all manner of sea-craft and boats are present around San Francisco Bay both at night and by day, they could easily have been picked up by a drifting boat waiting for a signal from a homemade light, then taken under the Golden Gate and put ashore to be picked up by a car. The raft and other materials may have been abandoned purposely, to give the impression they had followed the fate of others and drowned.

If they received no assistance but had still made the mainland, it would have been reasonable to assume they would either have resurfaced to commit crimes – though no unsolved robberies, car thefts or burglaries can be attributed to them – or to contact family and friends. Police and FBI monitoring over the years turned up nothing, though members of the family have admitted that signs had been received which led them to believe they survived. It was thought that they would go to Mexico, at least initially, all three of them having studied Spanish in prison.

West said that the plan had been to use the raft to make their way to Angel Island, and from there to re-enter the bay on the opposite side of the island and swim through a waterway called Raccoon Straits, before going on into Marin.

Saving face, as always, one officer later noted, "We never said it was *impossible* to escape from Alcatraz, only that it would be *very difficult* to escape from Alcatraz."

And yet, periodically over the years, the theory has been put to the test in such a way as to prove it, if not impossible, then extremely difficult. Various teams try to construct rafts in the same manner as the escapees, waiting for the climatic conditions of that fateful night to be repeated, in an effort to disprove the escape. Each time they select strong volunteers (usually in wetsuits in case they get too cold) who make bold attempts and then retire to safety – probably to have a good stiff drink before a nice warm fire. Usually very fit and well-fed professionals, they all seem to fail so miserably. And yet two points keep recurring each time one reads about these attempts.

First, why is it that, since the prison has closed, it has become a regular sport for people of all ages – from children to old people, from professionals to amateurs with little swimming ability – to swim out to or back from 'the Rock'? (Perhaps people are healthier today, but this is by no means universal.)

Second, even if the conditions were ice-cold and the currents strong (though it is believed they were not exceptionally strong on that night), men who are determined to escape are still in a cathartic state. These are men who have sat in their cells for weeks, months, years, with even more years ahead of them, and have thought long and hard about the risks of escaping; these are men for whom there is little else that life has to offer, little or nothing to lose; these are men who are at the limits; these are men who might walk on hot coals without burning their feet.

Some of these men may well flounder in the water, but others would override those factors and make it, whether to a waiting boat or dry land. If the raft should fail, then swimming and drifting would be their next recourse. The inadequacies of the ordinary person do not equate with the spirit, determination and ultimate *recklessness* of those hell-bent on escape.

They are not playing for the camera. They MUST escape. And things happen when MUST is the only option. If there is one thing that we can learn from the accounts in this book, and from those I have spoken to who have been on the E-List and escaped, it is the sheer force of that MUST that lifts the escapee beyond the limitations of possible and impossible.

Bibliography

Abagnale, Frank, *Catch Me If You Can* (Mainstream, 2001)

Ackroyd, Peter, *London* (Chatto & Windus, 2000)

Ball, John, Chester, Lewis and Perrott, Roy, *Cops and Robbers* (Penguin, 1979)

Bean, J. P., *Over the Wall* (Headline, 1994)

Becker, Jillian, *Hitler's Children* (Panther, 1978)

Biggs, Ronald, *Odd Man Out* (Bloomsbury, 1994)

Bourke, Seán, *The Springing of George Blake* (Cassell, 1970)

Brandon, David, *Stand & Deliver* (Sutton Publishing, 2001)

Bronson, Charles, *Bronson* (John Blake, 2006)

Bronson, Charles, *The Good Prison Guide* (John Blake, 2007)

Cabell, Craig, *The Kray Brothers* (Robson, 2002)

Campbell, Duncan, *That Was Business, This Is Personal* (Mandarin, 1990)

Carlson, Wayne, *Breakfast with the Devil* (Insomniac Press, 2001)

Casanova, Giacomo, *History of My Life: Volume Four* (Harcourt, Brace & World, 1967)

Chesney, Kellow, *The Victorian Underworld* (Maurice Temple Smith, 1970)

Clarkson, Wensley, *Bindon* (John Blake, 2005)

Clarkson, Wensley, *Costa del Crime* (John Blake, 2004)

Clarkson, Wensley, *Kenneth Noye: Public Enemy Number One*
(John Blake, 2006)

Clarkson, Wensley, *Killing Charlie* (Mainstream Publishing, 2004)

Clarkson, Wensley, *Moody* (Mainstream, 2003)

Cohen, Stanley and Taylor, Laurie, *Psychological Survival*
(Penguin, 1972)

Dark, Vic, *How to Rob Banks & Influence People* (John Blake, 2004)

DeNevi, Don, *Riddle of the Rock* (Promethus Books, 1991)

Donoghue, Albert and Short, Martin, *The Enforcer*
(John Blake, 2001)

Foreman, Freddie and Lambrianou, Tony, *Getting It Straight*
(Sidgwick & Jackson, 2001)

Foreman, Freddie, *Brown Bread Fred* (John Blake, 2007)

Fraser, Frankie with Morton, James, *Mad Frank's London*
(Virgin, 2001)

Fraser, Frankie with Morton, James, *Mad Frank and Friends*
(Little, Brown & Co, 1998)

Fraser, Frankie with Morton, James, *Mad Frank's Britain*
(Virgin, 2002)

Gaute, J. H. H. and Odell, Robin, *The New Murderers' Who's Who*
(Harrap, 1989)

Girardin, G. Russell with Helmer, William J., *Dillinger*
(Indiana University Press, 1994)

Hamilton, Lenny and Cabell, Craig, *Getting Away with Murder*
(John Blake, 2006)

Hamilton, Lenny, *Branded* (John Blake, 2002)

Hayes, Paddy, *Break-Out!* (O'Brien Press, 2004)

Hinds, Alfred, *Contempt of Court* (Panther, 1971)

Holland, Jimmy, *Scottish Hard Bastards* (John Blake, 2007)

Prison Break

Howard, Roger, *Great Escapes and Rescues*
  (Checkmark Books, 2001)
James, Trevor, *"There's One Away"* (Orchard Publications, 1999)
Keeton, G. W., *Guilty but Insane* (Macdonald, 1961)
Kelland, Gilbert, *Crime in London* (Grafton Books, 1987)
King, Patrick and Gates, Tudor, *Kidnapping Biggs*
  (Allison & Busby, 2006)
Knight, Ronnie, *Blood and Revenge* (John Blake, 2004)
Kray, Kate, *Killers* (John Blake, 2002)
Kray, Kate, *Ultimate Hard Bastards* (John Blake, 2005)
Kray, Reg, *A Way of Life* (Sidgwick & Jackson, 2000)
Lambrianou, Chris, *Escape from the Kray Madness*
  (Sidgwick & Jackson, 1995)
Linebaugh, Peter, *The London Hanged* (Verso, 2003)
Linnane, Fergus, *The Encyclopaedia of London Crime and Vice*
  (Sutton Publishing, 2003)
London, Sondra (editor), *Knockin' on Joe* (Nemesis, 1993)
Lucas, Norman, *The Child Killers* (Barker, 1970)
McVicar, John, *McVicar by Himself* (Arrow Books, 1979)
Michaud, Stephen, and Aynesworth, Hugh, *The Only Living Witness*
  (New English Library, 1989)
Moore, Lucy, *Con Men and Cutpurses* (Allen Lane, 2000)
Morton, James and Parker, Gerry, *Gangland Bosses*
  (Time Warner Books, 2004)
Morton, James, *Gangland Today* (Time Warner, 2002)
Morton, James, *Supergrasses and Informers*
  (Little, Brown & Co, 1995)
Neustatter, W. Lindesay, *The Mind of the Murderer*
  (Christopher Johnson, 1957)
O'Faolain, Nuala, *The Story of Chicago May* (Michael Joseph, 2005)
Parker, Norman, *Parkhurst Tales* (Smith Gryphon, 1994)

Pearson, John, *The Cult of Violence* (Orion, 2001)

Pearson, John, *The Profession of Violence* (Panther, 1973)

Priestley, Philip, *Jail Journeys* (Routledge, 1989)

Probyn, Walter, *Angel Face* (Allen & Unwin, 1977)

Progl, Zoe, *Woman of the Underworld* (Arthur Barker, 1964)

Quétel, Claude *Escape from the Bastille* (Polity Press, 1990)

Read, Piers Paul, *The Train Robbers* (W. H. Allen, 1978)

Reynolds, Bruce, *The Autobiography of a Thief* (Virgin, 2005)

Richardson, Charlie, *My Manor* (Pan, 1992)

Schofield, Carey, *Mesrine* (Penguin, 1980)

Sereny, Gitta, *Cries Unheard* (MacMillan, 1998)

Sifakis, Carl, *A Catalogue of Crime* (Signet, 1979)

Sifakis, Carl, *The Encyclopedia of American Crime*
    (Facts on File Inc, 1982)

Smith, Razor, *A Few Kind Words and a Loaded Gun* (Viking, 2004)

Smith, Razor, *Raiders* (Penguin, 2007)

Smith, Terry, *The Art of Armed Robbery* (John Blake, 2005)

Thomas, Donald, *The Victorian Underworld* (John Murray, 1998)

Wilson, Colin and Pitman, Pat, *Encyclopaedia of Murder* (Arthur
    Barker, 1961)

Wilson, Colin and Seaman, Donald, *Encyclopaedia of Modern Murder
    1962-1983* (Pan, 1986)

Wisbey, Marilyn, *Gangster's Moll* (Time Warner, 2002)

Every single case in this book was explored and counterchecked against websites too numerous to list.

Index of Escapees, Would-Be Escapees, and (Named) Associates